GROWTH
Has No Boundaries

THE CHRISTIAN'S SECRET TO
A DEEPER SPIRITUAL LIFE

DR. HENRY CLOUD
DR. JOHN TOWNSEND
Authors of *Boundaries*

ZONDERVAN

Growth Has No Boundaries
© 2001 by Henry Cloud and John Townsend

Derived from material previously published in *How People Grow*.
Abridgment by Kris Bearss.

Requests for information should be addressed to:
Zondervan, *3900 Sparks Dr. SE, Grand Rapids, Michigan 49546*

ISBN 978-0-785-23066-3 (hardcover)
ISBN 978-0-310-10821-4 (ebook)

Published in association with Yates & Yates, LLP, www.yates2.com.

Cover design: Jamie DeBruyn
Interior design: Emily Ghattas

Printed in the United States of America

19 20 21 22 23 24 25 26 27 28 / LSC / 10 9 8 7 6 5 4 3 2 1

Contents

PART I

Paradise Lost

CHAPTER 1

Harder Than
I THOUGHT

I t was my first day on the job in a Christian psychiatric hospital. I (Henry) was like a kid on Christmas
morning. I had been taking college and seminary classes
and reading all I could about Christian counseling for
about four years, and I was ready to put my knowledge
into practice. I showed up at the medical center in Dallas
early, all geared up to teach the patients how to find the
life I knew awaited them as soon as they learned the truth
I had been taught.

The unit was bustling with early-morning activity. I
saw patients talking with their doctors, nurses taking
patients' vital signs, and groups beginning their sessions—
the typical activities of a busy psychiatric unit.

I looked down the hall, and a woman in a pink

bathrobe walked out of her room. She extended her arms outward and exclaimed, "I am Mary, Mother of God!"

Here I am, brand new at Christian counseling, and thinking that all I had to do was come in and tell people God loved them, and if they would understand more of what he has said, they would be well. But when I heard what this woman said, I thought: *This is going to be harder than I thought.* It was a thought I would have many times in the year to come.

Four Models of How People Grow

In Christian circles at the time, there were basically four popular ways of thinking about personal growth: the sin model, the truth model, the experiential model, and the supernatural model.

The sin model said that all problems are a result of one's sin. If you struggled in your marriage or with an emotional problem such as depression, the role of the helper was to find the sin and confront you, urging you to confess, repent, and sin no more. If you did that, you were sure to get better.

The truth model held that the truth would set you free. If you were not "free," if some area of your life were not working, it must be because you lacked "truth" in your life. So the helper's role was to urge you to learn more verses and more doctrine (particularly your "position in

Christ"), and then all this truth would make its way from your head to your heart, and ultimately into your behavior and emotions.

The experiential model held that you had to find the abuse or the hurt in your life and then, in a kind of emotional archaeology, dig it up and seek healing through prayer or imagery or just clearing out the pain. Proponents of the more spiritual versions of this model either took the pain to Jesus or took Jesus to the pain.

The supernatural model had many variations. Charismatics sought instant healing and deliverance; others depended on the Holy Spirit to make the change happen as he lived his life through them. Exchanged-life people (those who hold that you just get out of the way so Christ can reproduce his life in you) trusted God to lead them and make changes in them.

While I saw value in and practiced all four models to some degree, it wasn't difficult for me to decide which one made the most sense. After all, I was heavily into theology and studying the Bible. So I found the most truth in the truth model. I believed in the power of the Bible and knew that God's truth could change any life.

Yet, at the medical center, I saw people who had walked with God for years, and many who knew more about God's truth than I did. These people had been very diligent about prayer, Bible study, and other spiritual disciplines. Nevertheless, they were hurting, and for one reason or another, they had been unable to walk through their valley.

3

The woman in the pink bathrobe was a missionary who had been called off the field because she was out of touch with who she was and where she was in time. She and hundreds of other clients that I encountered had tried the things they had been taught for dealing with marital, parenting, emotional, and work struggles, and they felt as though these spiritual answers had let them down.

It wasn't that people weren't gaining some relief through these methods. I often saw people improve, and prayer, learning Scripture, and repentance were very powerful elements in healing many clinical conditions. But something was missing. The feeling that "there has to be more" nagged at me.

Being Born Again, Again

I continued to work in Christian counseling, and something happened in the next four to five years that turned my world upside down: *I saw people grow past their stuck places.* Instead of depressed people coping better with depression, I saw depressed people become un-depressed. Instead of people with relational problems coping better, I saw them grow in their ability to make relationships work. I saw processes that actually changed people's lives. But they were paths of growth I had never been taught. So I was faced with a dilemma.

It seemed to me that there was the spiritual life, where

we learned about God and grew in our relationship to him, and then there was the emotional and relational life, where we learned how to solve real-life problems.

But it made no sense to me that there were answers other than spiritual ones. My theology taught me that God answers all of life's problems (2 Peter 1:3). How could there be spiritual growth and then other growth? Didn't it make sense that spiritual growth should be influencing these functional areas of life as well as the spiritual ones?

I had to find the answer to this problem; I could not live the life of a counselor helping people with problems, and then the life of a Christian, with a spiritual life that had value but did not solve the problems for which my clients were coming to me. Therefore I studied the Bible again to discover: How does spiritual growth address and solve life's problems?

The only way I know how to describe what happened at this point is to say that I was born again, again. Here is what happened: *I saw that everything I had been learning that helped people grow was right there in the Bible all along.* All the processes that had changed peoples' lives were in the pages of Scripture. The Bible talked about the things that helped people grow in relational and emotional areas as well as spiritual ones. I was ecstatic. Not only was the Bible true, but also what was true was in the Bible!

I saw it as my mission to communicate what I was

learning, so I began to teach workshops in Christian organizations. About the same time, John Townsend and I began talking through some of the same questions.

We had met in graduate school when I volunteered to help new students move in. Strangely, we became friends through our mutual love of rock music. At the time it was really un-Christian to like rock music, so we were both glad to find a friend who did not see the other as pagan. I found out that John had been on a similar quest himself and was passionate about the same goal. We wanted to bring all the issues for which people went to counseling back under the umbrella of spiritual growth, where they belonged.

We were not against counseling. People need to get into a context where they can work on their issues in-depth with an experienced counselor. But we had two emphases we cared about deeply.

First, when people came to us for counseling, we wanted them to understand that the issues they were working on were not *growth* issues or *counseling* issues, but *spiritual growth* issues. Spiritual growth, in our minds, was the answer to everything. Second, we wanted to bring the idea of working on relational and emotional issues back into the mainstream of spiritual growth.

There is no such thing as our "spiritual life" and then our "real life." Growth has no boundaries! It is all one.

We decided to address our concerns in three ways.

1. John and I wanted those responsible for helping people grow to know *how* the spiritual and the practical are linked. We wanted pastors to know, for example, how a small-group ministry that addresses people's emotional problems is an important application of the doctrine of the church, not just a good idea from secular humanism.

2. We wanted those who were working with people to be aware of the processes and skills that deeply change people's lives. Many do a great job in working with people in the things they have been exposed to, but, like us, have a longing to know more of what the Bible teaches about what makes people grow.

3. We wanted people who were growing to know not only how to grow, but to understand that "if you are getting better, it is because you are growing spiritually." It is good to know that growth is from God.

As we thought about the best way to write this book from a biblical perspective, we remembered how helpful our early roots in systematic theology and doctrine were. Therefore we would like, as best we can, to link the great doctrines of the Bible with how people grow spiritually, emotionally, and relationally.

Our desire is that the book be practical, that it help you understand how to help people grow *without putting any limits on God's work.* And, we want it to be a book that enlightens you on *how the growth process, at its very core, is theological.*

Back To Seminary

In theology, the Bible is broken up into categories that teach the major doctrines of the faith. We will go through some of the major categories of Christian doctrine, but we will spin them a little differently. We will not try to do an exhaustive study on the doctrines, but instead we will talk about *how each doctrine applies to personal growth.* We won't even always call them doctrines, but you can rest assured that the major doctrines of the faith are the architecture of this book, as they are the architecture of all that we do.

By the end of this book, we hope that you will be encouraged not only that growth can occur in very deep and significant ways, but also that those ways are the path of spiritual growth the Bible lays out for us. To us, that is an exciting journey—one that we relish every day. So join us as we take a look at what the Bible reveals about how people grow.

CHAPTER 2

Seeing The BIG PICTURE

Many times, in the process of helping people restore emotional health, heal a marriage, or make life work, we forget the big picture of what God is doing in the human race. But there really *is* a big picture! It is the story of God and his creation that was lost, and of his work to restore it to himself.

The apostle Paul said, "All this is from God, who reconciled us to himself through Christ and gave us the ministry of reconciliation: that God was reconciling the world to himself in Christ, not counting people's sins against them. And he has committed to us the message of reconciliation" (2 Cor. 5:18–19). This "message of reconciliation" is at the heart of the gospel. In salvation and in the growth process, God is reconciling things, bringing them back to the way they should be.

Many times we forget the way things should be, and what we are trying to accomplish in helping people grow. We zero in on the "problem" that someone needs help with, such as depression or intimacy, as though this problem were the main issue. Or we hammer in on a pattern of behavior we think is the sin behind the struggle, and we think that if we can get the person to be good enough, then we have helped him or her.

In the counseling arena, and when we preach, teach, disciple, or encourage people to engage in spiritual disciplines, we speak to problems and "symptoms," and we miss the real life-changing dynamics of this "ministry of reconciliation." After all, it is far easier to focus on a particular problem in someone's life, or to focus on how someone is "missing the mark," than it is to figure out the ways that the Fall is still operative in the person's life and discover a redemptive path that will "reconcile" his or her life.

But the call to address the root issue is exactly the call we have received. We are not just to help others "feel better" or relate better or perform better. And God forbid, we are not just to try to get them to "do better." This is the essence of the pharisaical life. We are to be working with God as he reconciles all things to himself.

The question then becomes "What are we trying to reconcile?" We are obviously trying to get people back into a relationship with God. But beyond that, we are trying to reconcile people to each other, and to the idea of holiness and pure living. Great life change and healing are to be had when these three things occur.

Spiritual growth is also about *coming back to life*—the life that God created for people to live. We must be reconciled to life the way it was created to work.

To get us started, I (Henry) would like to look at three big acts in the cosmic drama: Creation, the Fall, and Redemption. If we are going to deeply help people on the path to spiritual growth, we have to look at the way God created life to begin with, what happened to that life, and what God has said about getting it back.

Act One: Creation

Big Idea Number One: God Is the Source

In the beginning there was God, and God created the heavens and the earth. *Everything starts out with God as the Source.* This is point number one in the Bible, and this is point number one in our theology of growth. Nothing was in creation before God, and everything that exists came from him. This includes all the "stuff" of life—the resources, the principles, the purposes, the meaning—everything. He is the Source, period.

After making the "stuff," God made humankind; he created Adam and Eve. And he breathed life into them (Gen. 2:7). So as you think about restoring life, remember that life came from God. We all think we know that, but we tend to mean by it merely that God created life from non-life. But if we are in the process of helping people grow, we have to understand that it includes his bringing life to dead situations in our lives. It becomes the theology of how one overcomes a depression or heals a marriage or rescues a failing business career. In other words, "How do I bring this marriage or this business career back to life?"

The Bible's answer to all these questions is "God." There is a Person behind it all who will create and give us life and growth.

Big Idea Number Two: Relationship

The second big idea is that when God created humans, he put them into relationship, first with him and then with each other. We have already seen that Adam depended on a relationship with God for life. But even with that relationship, he needed human connection as well. As God said, "It is not good for the man to be alone" (Gen. 2:18).

An important aspect of this relationship is that there was no "brokenness" in either Adam and Eve's relationship with God or in their relationship with each other. As the Bible says, "Adam and his wife were both naked, and they felt no shame" (v. 25). They were laid bare before one another, and there was neither shame nor hiding. There was no fighting or bickering. There was harmony and vulnerability between the man and the woman. Relationship experts speak of this state as "intimacy," where people are known at deep levels. One of the aspects of genuine, healthy relatedness is that people are not ashamed of who they are before each other. Relationship as it was created to be was vulnerable and open, without duplicity and without brokenness or breach.

Big Idea Number Three: God Is the Boss

Relationships were not just tossed in a bowl like a salad. There was an order to them. First of all, in the relationship between God and humans, God was the Boss, the Lord, the Authority. Adam and Eve's order and position in creation was to take care of the garden and obey God. It was a high position, but it also had limits. They were to work in the land that God had given them, they were to enjoy it, and they were to submit to God and his limits.

Early on, creation involved a "good life" and a "prohibited life" (which is an oxymoron, since the prohibited life would result in death). We were to live life in submission to God, or we would not have life at all. Life and submission to God were one and the same.

Big Idea Number Four: Roles of God, Roles of People

God is the Boss, and we are to obey. But there is more to this structure than just "who's on top." We were to have distinctly different roles in this order of creation.

1. **God's role was to be the source or provider; our role was to depend on the source.** If God is the Creator and we are the creation, we have to depend on him for life and provision. Independence is not an option for us. God existed without us, not vice versa. So the role that we must take in life is not only *for* dependency, but also *against* self-sufficiency. Our role is to recognize our limits and to transcend those limits by looking *outside of ourselves* for life. Thus we are limited in our ability to live alone, apart from God.

   Self-sufficiency from God is not the only relational limit we have. We also need other people and cannot live independently from them either. The results of trying to live apart from our need for others are disastrous. *We must depend on the outside for love.*

2. **God's role was to be in control; our role was to yield to God's control of the world and to control our self.** God had done the creating; God had placed Adam and Eve in the garden; God created the animals and the various trees and their fruits. Humans did not. In other words, God was in charge of the big picture.

   So, not only were we dependent on God for these things, but we were not in any particular position to run the universe either. As God said to Job later, "Where were you when I laid the earth's foundation? Tell me, if you understand"

(Job 38:4). But we did have control of our own behavior, and we were to exercise that responsibly. God's role is to be in control of the big picture, and our role is to be in control of our self and our responsibilities. In short, to maintain "self-control."

3. **God was the judge of life; we were to experience life.** Another role that belonged to God was to know good from evil. He sat in the judge's chair, and he did not want humans to know what he knew about evil. So God commanded Adam and Eve to stay away from the tree of the knowledge of good and evil and to let him be God. We were to live the good life apart from judging it. Imagine that: we were to experience all that God had given us in pleasure, work, and relationship. Live it to all the limits, but remain innocent and not even know that we were innocent. God alone was judge, and in essence he said to us, "Don't assume that role."

4. **God made the rules; we were to obey them.** God did not consult us on setting up the rules and the design of life. He did not ask us if our ruling over animals was a good idea, or if he had chosen the right trees to give us to eat, or if we thought man and woman was a good idea. He did not ask us whether having to work was a good idea. He just made the reality and then told us to obey it.

The Whole Package

If you think about it, this was pretty much the life everyone is looking for: a great place to live, the perfect mate, lots of good things to occupy your time, and a job that fits your makeup.

If these things had remained in place, there would be no need for this book. We would still be in the garden experiencing life as it was designed, and we would not even be aware of what life would look like any other way. But instead of remaining the innocent crown of creation, we took a great tumble, which brings us to Act Two.

Act Two: The Fall

Reversing the Order

The next act in the cosmic drama happened after creation. The Tempter came along and got Adam and Eve to reverse the entire created order by rebelling against what God had said. He questioned the truth of what God had told them and said they would not really die if they ate of the fruit from the tree of knowledge of good and evil. In fact, they would become like God himself. In essence, they could be to themselves all that God was to have been to them.

But, as we all know, this was a lie. The man and woman did not become like God at all. *Instead, in trying to become God, they became less of themselves.* And this is why we need spiritual growth. We have become less of what we were created to be.

Although they were still human, Adam and Eve "fell" from the perfect state they were created in, and were now in a strange state that the Bible calls "sin" or "death" (Eph. 2:1). To sin means to "miss the mark," and death means to be separated from life, especially "separated from the life of God" (Eph. 4:18).

In short, they lost it all. They lost themselves, each other, and the life they were created to have. They overturned the entire design. And look at what happened.

1. **They became independent from the source.** When Adam and Eve ate from the tree, they moved away from God and tried to gain life apart from him. They thought they could get knowledge and wisdom apart from the Source. They no longer needed him and took a step away from their role of dependency.

2. **They lost their relationships.** They lost their relationship with him as well as with each other. This is what death is. When God said they would die, he meant that they would be separated from him who is life. They went into a state of what the Bible refers to as "alienation," actually becoming "enemies" of God (Col. 1:21). The relationship

and intimacy they had with their Creator was lost; they became separated from him.

They also lost their other primary relationship, the one with each other. Instantly they became "naked and ashamed" and covered themselves with fig leaves. Their intimacy and vulnerability was lost, as was their ability to trust each other. From that point on, we see humans trading trust, fairness, love, and honesty with each other for alienation, unfairness, adversarial relationships, and dishonesty. Love became much harder to find and sustain.

3. **They reversed the structure.** In the creation, God was on top, and Adam and Eve answered to his authority. He was the lord, the ruler. But in the Fall, humans tried to usurp that structure and become their own lord. They tried to become "like God." In short, they became self-sufficient, controlling people who were judgmental and lived by their own rules.

4. **They reversed the roles.** Adam and Eve tried to become God, and in the process they lost their ability to be what only they could be: themselves. And we have been searching for ourselves ever since.

But God did not allow things to stay that way. He had another plan.

Act Three: Redemption

God in Christ is "reconciling" all things. He redeemed his creation and is putting it all back in place. How did he do this?

God paid the price. The holy God required the death penalty for the sin of humankind. And as the Bible tells us, he laid all of this sin upon Jesus (Isa. 53:5–6). This paved the way for God to return everything to its rightful order. And this is what redemption does for each and every human who applies it to his or her life. This application of redemption is the process of growth itself: it is the returning of everything to its rightful, "righteous" place before God. In redemption we reconcile things to the way they were supposed to be.

- We become dependent and give up our independent stance before God and others.
- We give up trying to control things we cannot control and trust God's control. Also, we regain control of what we were created to control in the first place, which is our self. We regain the fruit of "self-control."
- We give up the role of playing judge with ourselves and others by giving up condemnation, wrath, shaming, and so on. By not being God, we are free to be who we truly are and allow others to be who they truly are as well.

- We stop redesigning life and making new rules and instead live the life God designed us to live. In redemption, we begin to do things God's way.

Moving Past The Beginning

In Hebrews 6:1–3 we find the following statements:

> Therefore let us move beyond the elementary teachings about Christ and be taken forward to maturity, not laying again the foundation of repentance from acts that lead to death, and of faith in God, instruction about cleansing rites, the laying on of hands, the resurrection of the dead, and eternal judgment. And God permitting, we will do so.

The writer has gone to a lot of trouble to explain the elementary teachings about Christ, and he wants people to go on from there to maturity, or "completeness." But to make life work, we must remember two things. First, there are foundational principles without which nothing else works. If we do not order *our* growth and the growth of *the ones we minister to* according to these foundational things, we are building on quicksand. Second, there is a process that takes us from the "foundation" to "maturity." So often we either learn the elementary things and over time forget them, or we try to make the elementary things the entire picture of growth.

John and I contend that in order for "growth that makes life work" and for people to come to "completeness," both things must occur. We must order growth according to a firm foundation, and we must also build on the foundation with the rest of God's provision. We must have the basics in place and then go beyond the basics.

In the following chapters we will both show God's foundation and how to use it, and also move "foward to maturity" by looking at the rest of the story beyond the foundation. Join us now as we begin that journey.

PART II

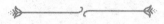

The Master Gardener

CHAPTER 3

The God of
GRACE

It was the spring of my sophomore year at Southern Methodist University, and I (Henry) remember that Sunday afternoon as if it were yesterday. I was at the end of myself.

I had been recruited to play NCAA golf, and I was pursuing my lifelong dream of competitive play. I'd had significant success as a teenage amateur, but in my freshman year I began to have severe on-again, off-again pain in the tendons of my left hand. I went to many doctors to find out what was causing the pain, but they were stumped.

The next two years I played through the pain, but my game never was the same. Finally, I decided to quit.

I found myself in one of those times of life when a door has been slammed shut, and I did not see another one open. I wondered what to do next. I looked at various interests and majors, only to arrive at a sense of darkness regarding the future.

My relational future did not look any more hopeful than my vocational one. I had many friends, but a few failed dating relationships had left me wondering if I would ever be able to make a relationship work.

It was in this state of mind and circumstance that I found myself that Sunday afternoon in my room. As I sat on my bed thinking about all the aspects of life that were not working, I looked up at my bookshelf and noticed a Bible. I had not read the Bible since I had left for college. Nevertheless, something drew me to that Book, and I picked it off the shelf and randomly opened it. A verse jumped off the page: "But seek first his kingdom and his righteousness, and all these things will be given to you as well" (Matt. 6:33).

This verse hit me like a light. "All these things" was exactly what I was worried about.

I then noticed a verse above that one: "I tell you, do not worry about your life, what you will eat or drink; or about your body, what you will wear. Is not life more important than food, and the body more important than clothes?" (v. 25).

And then the kicker: "Therefore do not worry about tomorrow, for tomorrow will worry about itself. Each day has enough trouble of its own" (v. 34).

I was hit hard by a reality that I did not at that moment

understand, but I knew that these words spoke to me. Was it true that all of these things would be given to me if I sought God? I did not even know God provided things for people. But I was hit hard enough to want to give it a try.

So I took a walk, and I made a decision. I would seek God's righteousness and see if it worked. I would "seek God." But I really didn't know how, so I did the only thing I could think of—I found the empty Highland Park Chapel on the SMU campus, and I went to the front and said a simple prayer: "God, I don't even know if you are there. But if you are and you can do this, then show me, and I will do whatever you tell me to do."

Nothing happened. I went back to my room, wondering if anything would come of my having reached out to God.

Later, the phone rang. It was a fraternity brother. What he said stunned me: "I don't know why I thought of you, but we are starting a Bible study at my apartment, and I wanted to see if you would like to come."

Without explaining why, I simply said, "I'll be there."

I went to that Bible study. And there I found that what I had read that day in the Bible had been more true than I ever could have imagined: the answers to life and all of its issues are found in seeking God *and* his righteousness. What I did not know was that both the seeking and the righteousness would be a long process.

In this chapter we take a look at how a relationship

with God "grows life." We will look at concepts that might seem elementary to some—but ones that we need to be continually reminded of—and at how those concepts help us grow.

A True View of God

I have been amazed—in my own life as well as in the lives of others—at how unnatural it is for us to see God as he really is. In fact, one of Jesus' main emphases when he walked the earth was to show people what God was really like.

People do not grow until they shift from a natural, human view of God to a real, biblical view of God. *The first aspect of that shift has to be the shift from a God of law to the God of grace. People must discover that God is for them and not against them.*

Many Christians misunderstand grace. Usually people think that grace means forgiveness or the absence of condemnation. But while forgiveness is an expression of the grace of God, grace is much bigger. Theologically, grace is *unmerited favor*. This definition has two important implications:

1. Favor means that God is on our side and desires good for us and not evil.
2. His favor cannot be earned, and even if it could

be, we do not have the means to earn it. Therefore he will freely give us things we cannot provide for ourselves.

Practically, these two implications of grace undergird the entire growth process. To grow, we need things that we do not have and cannot provide, and we need to have a source of those things who looks favorably upon us and who does things for us for our own good. The Bible teaches that if we have faith in God, we are in an entire life situation of grace. This contrasts with being in a life situation of law.

Paul contrasts the phrase "under the law" with being "under grace" (see Rom. 6:14–15; Gal. 4:4–5; 5:18). When we are under the law—in our natural state—we feel that God is the enemy and that we get what we deserve. We naturally try to "earn" life. We are trying to "save ourselves" (see Matt. 16:25). We try to get God to not be mad, and to grow and resolve our issues by our own efforts. Yet Paul says that this way of living is the exact opposite of living according to faith and grace (Gal. 3:11).

This is not just theology; it is exactly how people end up living out their real-life problems until they grasp the reality of grace. And the result is failure. Watch how it works in a real example.

I recently talked with a minister-friend who was try-ing to help another friend, whom we'll call Dirk, lose about a hundred pounds. Dirk had decided that he needed to make a commitment to God and to his friend to lose the weight, and he was going to go on a diet to that end. Dirk was to be accountable to my friend to check in every few months to see how he was doing with his plan.

When Dirk checked in, his weight had gone up.

When my friend confronted him about the seriousness of the situation, Dirk responded as someone living under the law: "I know. I've failed, and I feel terrible. I'm such a sinner. I'll ask God for forgiveness, and I'll do better. I'll really commit this time, not only to sticking to a diet, but also to exercising. I promise to do better."

I told my friend that I could guarantee that Dirk was headed for another failure until he revised his whole belief system. He was still under the law and not in grace. First, he felt that God was angry at him for his failure, and therefore he wallowed in guilt. Second, he still thought that he could earn his way out of his problem by "trying harder."

What would have been a grace response?

First, Dirk would see that God was more interested in his getting healthy than he was. He would see a God that he could turn to for help in his time of need (Heb. 4:16). Grace teaches that God views our inability as a part of reality, and he is not mad at our weakness. In fact, he calls our being unable to do what we need to do a "blessed" state (Matt. 5:3; 2 Cor. 12:9–10).

Second, because of that view, Dirk would see that he was unable to lose weight by his own efforts and that help was going to have to come from the outside. The God of grace would not ask him to do it all on his own. He would provide support, mentors, coaches, and other people who could help him. He would also give him his own power to strengthen him. This is very different than "self-help." The God of grace is a God who helps.

When we first look at having a view of God that affects growth, we must begin with grace. This "grace" is God's provision of various resources and tools to help us grow. We do not grow because of willpower or self-effort; God offers the help we need, and then we must respond to that provision.

Practical Theology

Understanding grace is not just a theological exercise; it is essential to constructing a system of growth. So, first, make sure that your ministry is one that lets people know over and over again and in a thousand different ways that God is not their enemy, but one who wants to help. This also means understanding God as the source of life, not of rules.

Too often Christians who fail think of God as being someone they need to avoid instead of being the One they need to turn to. They are still "under the law" at a deep emotional level. Christians who fail also avoid other Christians, especially when they are feeling bad and guilty in the midst of failure.

In Twelve Step groups, people are taught that the very first thing to do when you fail is to call someone in the group and get to a meeting. They are taught to "run to grace," as it were—to turn immediately to their higher power and their support system. The sad part is that this theology is more biblical than what is practiced in many Christian environments.

Second, make sure that they are not subtly providing their own help. Dirk had to find the favors, the grace, and the resources from outside. He could not earn or create them.

Getting To The Need for Grace

Two things must happen in any ministry designed for growth. First, emphasis on the law must be eliminated. The law will make things worse, not better (Rom. 5:20; 7:10). It must be died to (Rom. 7:4; Gal. 2:19). It destroys any growth God has begun in someone's life. Second, we must help people realize their need for grace.

In the example at the beginning of this chapter, I experienced the death of all my dreams and of my ability to find a life that worked. By realizing my inability to live up to the laws of life, I was a candidate for unmerited favor. I realized that I was in need of God.

Sometimes we must help people get to a "death experience" for grace to take effect and growth to begin. (This is what addicts call "hitting bottom." Some call it "ego death.") We must let them, and sometimes help them, reach the end of themselves and find out that things are really bad. This is contrary to what many counselors, groups, and teachers do. We live in an age of people wanting to avoid pain, and sometimes we construct ministries geared to making people feel good about themselves.

John and I once felt very validated when a man told us, "I think I get it. The ministry I used to go to was into winning, and you guys are into losing." We had been talking to him about facing the fact that all his attempts at success and building "self-esteem" were taking him farther away from the answer to his problems. He had to get to a place where he faced how bad things really were; things were not going to get better until he saw that reality.

In your work with people, you have to be a funeral director, showing them that they need to die not only to the law, but also to themselves. All their efforts have not worked, and they need to die to trying. To get people to give up is very hard, but it must be done so that they can try God instead.

Helping Others Get To The Need for Grace

Confrontation

Although the law is useless as a change agent, it does have value. Its value is to show us our need for grace (Rom. 3:20; Gal. 3:24). For this reason it *is* important that the helping process include law, not as a way to get better, but *as a way to help people know their need.*

In other words, those who do not know their need must be confronted with their denial. Dirk was in denial of his need for grace; he still thought he could lose weight on his own. I told my friend that he was going to have to "lay down the law" for Dirk. He should say, "You are failing in your attempts to change, and you had better realize that you will not lose weight by trying harder. You need help."

Confrontation is an important tool to get someone to see his inability to change. Many people are too soft-hearted; they give *encouragement* to someone who needs *discouragement* instead. To encourage a powerless person to try harder is one of the worst things you could possibly do. The best thing you can do is to discourage him from believing that he can do it on his own.

Reality Consequences and Discipline

Too often in the church, we protect people from the logical consequences that would force them to see their need for grace and what it can provide. Either we feel

The God of Grace

sorry for them and bail them out, or we fear them and cater to them. The Bible warns against both: "'Do not pervert justice; do not show partiality to the poor or favoritism to the great, but judge your neighbor fairly'" (Lev. 19:15).

No matter what the person's plight, we must help him face the truth. It may mean letting them lose a job, or a relationship, or lose membership in a group or a fellowship. Those of us in positions of helping others grow must have the courage to allow people to experience those consequences, or else we may be keeping them from grace.

The story of the prodigal son in Luke 15 is an example. The son asked his father for his share of the estate. Certainly the father could have nagged, made offers, or become angry to persuade his younger son to change his mind. Who knows —maybe he did, but we are not given that information. What we do know is that the father allowed his son to choose and then to experience the consequences. The son, after receiving his share of the estate, set off for a distant country, where he squandered his wealth in wild living. After his money was gone, he was forced to feed pigs for a living.

These consequences of the son's own choices turned him around, helped him see his need, and put him in a position where he could receive the things his father had to offer. The pigsty was a correcting experience, thus a gift of grace.

So, in thinking about growth, leave room for people to fail. Sometimes you may even have to be the agent of failure, as in kicking someone out of a group or firing a staff member. Reality consequences are not all bad. They are part of God's plan.

CHAPTER 4

Jesus: Our Example
FOR LIVING

For the longest time in my life, I (John) didn't know where to put Jesus. As a child I can remember seeing God the Father as someone who could help me with things such as good grades, getting me out of trouble with my parents, and having my team win in baseball.

In college I learned about the Holy Spirit's ongoing ministry in my heart, and I studied Christ's sacrifice for my sins, giving me a righteous standing before God. But though I saw the Father and Spirit's roles in my spiritual growth, I didn't realize what the Son did beyond salvation.

Then, during my graduate studies in theology and psychology, I looked at the unique role Jesus plays in the spiritual growth process. As I did, I realized I could not imagine genuine spiritual maturity without the contributions of Jesus. That is the subject of this chapter. We will look at several specific areas in which Jesus helps people grow.

The Ongoing Relationship

First, Jesus is "with" us. Jesus has gone to be with the Father, but he also lives in the heart of each believer: "And surely I am with you always, to the very end of the age" (Matt. 28:20). By faith, he lives inside us, "so that Christ may dwell in your hearts through faith" (Eph. 3:17). This means we have an ongoing, sustaining relationship with him. In some mysterious way, Jesus and the Holy Spirit indwell us. In the Old Testament, God resided in the temple. Now *people* are the temple (1 Cor. 3:16). With Jesus we have a personal, living connection with God.

People need two sorts of relationships to grow: the divine and the human. If you are helping people grow, make sure you look for how connected they are to the indwelling Christ. No matter what the issue or struggle, relatedness must come first. It is as important as checking the gas gauge before you leave on a car trip.

Much of this process involves learning to become aware of Jesus. Our natural bent is to use only our five senses to experience this world and its realities. However, the Bible teaches that the spiritual reality is just as real as the physical world. Growers need to know that being aware, responsive, and dependent on Jesus is a daily part of life.

If you are a growth facilitator, you will often find that people who have been hurt in relationships may have difficulty trusting God or anyone else. Others may have become emotionally detached to the point they have become self-sufficient and insular. They are glad Jesus is there, but they don't know what to do with him. Still others may see him as dangerous, because they view all relationships that way.

Help growers see that God is good, that Jesus lives in the believer's heart, and that trusting relationship brings good things.

Identification

Another way Jesus is essential to spiritual growth is called *identification*. He serves as a model that can teach and comfort us in many growth situations. Biblical principles tell us how people grow; Jesus shows us. He gives us a personal and human example we can see and internalize within our hearts. We have a living, breathing picture of how God wants us to live. The bulk of this chapter will show those aspects of identification with Jesus that apply to people's growth.

Response To Suffering

One of the most important tasks of spiritual growth is to understand how to suffer. No one grows to maturity who does not understand suffering.

Normalize suffering. Jesus shows us much about how to respond to suffering. Most important is that he did not avoid suffering, but saw it as part of the growth path: "Son though he was, he learned obedience from what he suffered" (Heb. 5:8). He resolutely moved toward the pain ahead for him (Luke 9:51).

Jesus turns our natural bents upside down. In the world's view, the path to glory is "having it all together." In Jesus' way, the path to glory is experiencing pain and suffering: "Now if we are children, then we are heirs— heirs of God and co-heirs with Christ, if indeed we share in his sufferings in order that we may also share in his glory" (Rom. 8:17).

Choose Godly suffering. Sometimes people have difficulty understanding when they should suffer and when they should avoid it. Some suffering needs to be avoided (Prov. 22:3). Conversely, some people will avoid good pain for fear of conflict or abandonment.

Jesus is a wonderful example of embracing needful suffering and rejecting that which is not. He understood that pain must have a purpose. He chose the path of the cross because of the fruit it would bear for all of us. Yet he refused to enter suffering that would be inappropriate to his purposes (John 10:39).

Be humble. One way to bear necessary pain is to be humble. If we are humble, we will be willing to allow something uncomfortable to happen to us *if* it is the right thing to do. This is because part of being humble means not perceiving ourselves to have rights or privileges that we do not possess.

The opposite of humility is grandiosity, a defense mechanism that prevents us from suffering rightly. There are several types of grandiosity. Some people deny their experience, trying to be strong and saying, "This doesn't hurt me." Others insist their righteousness should prevent their suffering, saying, "Why me? I've been good." Still others attempt to avoid suffering altogether, saying, "Because this is uncomfortable, I will not experience it," and they thwart suffering's growth benefits.

Jesus' example is so instructive here. He could have rightfully claimed his divinity and avoided all he went through. Yet he "did not consider equality with God something to be used to his own advantage; rather, he made himself nothing by taking the very nature of a servant, being made in human likeness" (Phil. 2:6–7). Ultimately, he humbled himself and underwent pain he didn't bring on himself. This is a wonderful example for people in your growth groups. It will help them see the value of humility in suffering rightly.

Depend on God and people. While we must endure the work of growth, we can't bear it alone. Jesus was dependent on God and people. He taught us to be like him and ask God for our daily bread (Matt. 6:11). Yet he also asked his closest friends to be present with him in his dark hours (Matt. 26:38). We can't bear life on our own, nor were we created to. Jesus did not model independence, but dependence.

Submit to God's way. In the garden of Gethsemane, when Jesus realized that the time of his crucifixion was drawing near, he in deep anguish asked God for his suffering to end. He did not want to go through what he had to go through. Yet he submitted to the path God had placed before him and said, "Not my will, but yours be done" (Luke 22:42).

Jesus made the same choice when the Devil tempted him (Matt. 4:1–11). Satan first approached Jesus after he had fasted many days (v. 2) and told Christ to command the stones to become bread, so that he might eat. At a deeper level, this was a temptation to Jesus to get his needs met in ways other than God's. Jesus responded by going back to Scripture and confronting Satan with the reality that he could get his needs met God's way. The Devil then told Jesus to test God by throwing himself off a temple (vv. 5–6). This was a temptation to control God rather than to trust him and his ways. Jesus confronted that strategy also.

Finally, Satan offered Jesus all the kingdoms of the world for his worship (vv. 8–9). Had Jesus accepted, he would have not had to die on the cross. Yet he strongly rebuked the Devil. This was a temptation to avoid suffering. Jesus' response to this temptation is a living invitation for us to see that when we follow his path, we may suffer. However, that suffering is a small price to pay for the spiritual growth that results.

Response To Being Sinned Against

We bring a great deal of pain to our lives by our own transgressions (sins by us); at the same time, others inflict much injury on us (sins against us).

We have natural responses to being hurt that are part of our fallenness: Adam succumbed to temptation, then attempted to avoid responsibility for it (Gen. 3:9–12). These responses come easily but do not help us grow; however, Jesus, as the New Adam, provides a better way to look at injury that helps us grow closer to God and also grow in character. Here are some tools for the suffering caused by others.

Acknowledge the wound; don't deny it. Jesus never pretended hurtful things didn't hurt. In fact, he spoke to his disciples about his future suffering, which upset them greatly. They were horrified he was being so negative (Matt. 16:21–22)! Yet he knew they needed to understand the suffering he was to go through. If he had denied his pain, they (and we) would not have understood the cost of his sacrifice.

Growth facilitators need to help people open up about the realities of their past and present hurts. Jesus didn't pretend everything was okay when it wasn't.

Stay connected; don't isolate. We tend to withdraw from relationship when we are hurt. Some people are afraid of their dependencies on others. Others feel guilty about burdening friends with their problems. Still others try to be self-sufficient. None of these responses helps a person heal and grow.

In the garden of Gethsemane, during one of his darkest hours of preparing for the ultimate injury, Jesus asked for support from his friends: "My soul is overwhelmed with sorrow to the point of death. Stay here and keep watch with me'" (Matt. 26:38). Teach his example to those you are helping grow. Help them see that Jesus' way is not the way of detachment, but of emotional dependency on God and others.

Love and forgive; don't retaliate. We are by nature a people who have the law of retaliation in our hearts: an eye for eye and a tooth for tooth (Ex. 21:24). But Jesus taught and lived a greater principle: "I tell you, do not resist an evil person. If anyone slaps you on the right cheek, turn to them the other cheek also" (Matt. 5:39). His first response was not to extract revenge, but to give the other person a chance. This is quite "unnatural"; in fact, it is a work of God in someone's life to not retaliate against one who has wounded him or her.

Jesus' teaching on this subject confuses many people. They wonder if he is saying we should never protect ourselves from hurt. It is an important question. However, remember these two facts: (1) Jesus' words are true. We are called not to take revenge, but to make peace, which is a higher calling; and (2) the passage needs to be understood in the light of all of Scripture. Other passages teach us to protect ourselves also (Prov. 22:3). Thus we need to look at each situation individually and work out how to protect ourselves without vengeance.

Practice self-control; don't be controlled. Our getting hurt in a relationship is proof of how little control we have over others in the first place. Many times we transfer power onto the person who has hurt us, which makes things worse.

Jesus handled this in a different way. When others hurt him, Jesus didn't give control of his life to those who injured him, and he did not allow the hurt to change his values or direction in life. This trait is called self-control. He completed the tasks the Father had given him, and the last words he uttered before he died from his suffering were "It is finished" (John 19:30). He was in charge of his life to the end.

If you are a growth facilitator, help your people to develop self-control. While they need to confess and process pain, they also need to take back ownership of their lives rather than staying stuck and being controlled by the hurts of others.

Jesus' Identification with Our Suffering

There is another type of identification that deeply assists our growth. Jesus knows about our suffering through his own experience:

> Because he himself suffered when he was tempted, he is able to help those who are being tempted (Heb. 2:18).
>
> For we do not have a high priest who is unable to sympathize with our weaknesses, but we have one who has been tempted in every way, just as we are—yet he did not sin (Heb. 4:15).

Jesus put himself in a unique position by his suffering. If anyone can say about our situation, "I've been there," it is he. There are two key terms here: "help" and "sympathize." They point out that Jesus both assists us and feels compassion for us. If you have ever had a friend who wanted to help you but didn't understand you, or one who understood you but had no help for you, you see why it is so good that Jesus has both capacities in his identification with us.

The Greek word for "sympathize" means "commiserate." It indicates that Jesus "knows" our suffering at much more than an intellectual level, at a very personal one. Experience is the only gate through which he could have gained full knowledge of us, and he did it at a terrible cost.

If we know that someone truly understands, we know

we are not alone with our feelings and thoughts, and we gain encouragement to persevere in our growth. We need to know that we are "heard"—on a human level from each other, and on a divine level from God (Ps. 10:17). This is what Jesus' identification provides. When we realize that he "gets it" because of his own suffering, we are buoyed up and can continue down the path.

Another benefit of Jesus' identification with us is that it leaves us without excuse when we want to turn from God in our pain. If we can say, "No one truly understands my life," it helps us feel justified to stay out of the growth path. Jesus' suffering breaks through that obstacle and helps us repent of turning away from him and his healing ways.

God the Father and Jesus the Son both powerfully guide how people grow. In the next chapter, find out how the Holy Spirit is just as important in the process.

CHAPTER 5

The HOLY SPIRIT

What if Jesus came to your house today for a visit, and you told him you wanted to grow? What would you expect him to do? Heal you? Teach you? Challenge you? Give you new talents? I (Henry) can come up with many things I would expect him to do, but one of the last things I would expect him to say is, "Oh, you want to grow? Well, if that is what you want, I will have to leave. See you later."

But this is exactly what Jesus did: "But very truly I tell you, it is for your good that I am going away. Unless I go away, the Advocate will not come to you; but if I go, I will send him to you. . . . But when he, the Spirit of truth, comes, he will guide you into all the truth" (John 16:7, 13).

For reasons we do not fully understand, Jesus decided to go to heaven and work on us from there, and he sent the Holy Spirit to be with us and produce the growth and change we seek. And he said that this is better than his being here himself. Therefore all I can think is that it must be incredible to have the Holy Spirit in our lives.

Let's take a look at the ways the Holy Spirit is involved in the growth process.

The Initiator and the Completer

One of the first things you should teach people is that they can trust the growth process, no matter how they feel in the midst of it. It is not going to be only up to them to "make it." *The Spirit begins the process of growth by wooing us to Jesus, and he is working to finish the task* (Phil. 1:6). The Holy Spirit is always going to be there, drawing us to God and to greater and greater growth.

When I first began my path of growth, I wondered one day if God wanted to have anything to do with me anymore. I prayed, and my hurts and pains were not quickly going away. I thought God had left me.

In the midst of these thoughts I remember a pastor telling me, "If God were through with you, you would not be worried about it. The desire you feel for him and for growth can only come from him and his Spirit. If you are moving toward God, it's because he's moving toward you. Rest in this fact. If you want him, he is look-ing for you." Then he showed me John 6:44 to prove his point: "No one can come to me unless the Father who sent me draws them." I found out there is no such thing as "wanting God" and not being able to have him. If we want him, he is looking for us.

Security

In any relationship, to grow and change we have to first know we are secure. Our relationship with God is no different.

The Holy Spirit gives us this security. After bringing us to a relationship with God, he locks the door behind us. Just as Noah locked the door of the ark to save a rem-nant of life from the flood, the Holy Spirit locks the door of our saving "ship," our relationship with Jesus. Listen to what happens: "You also were included in Christ when you heard the message of truth, the gospel of your salva-tion. When you believed, you were marked in him with a seal, the promised Holy Spirit" (Eph. 1:13).

When we put our trust in Jesus, we enter the boat, so to speak, and the door is sealed behind us. Through the sealing work of the Holy Spirit, God himself protects us to be always his. This has wonderful implications for the growth process. Because of the work of the Holy Spirit, we can stop worrying about whether or not this relationship is secure, and we can get on with the work of growth.

The Partnership

Beyond the security and assurance the Spirit provides, what does the work of the Spirit look like day to day? What does he do? How do we work with him? As Jesus said, one way to think about the Holy Spirit is as the "Advocate." He is someone who comes alongside us and helps us. And the ways he helps are numerous. Here is a partial list of what we can expect to happen in the Christian life as we ask for and work with the Spirit:

- He will always be with us, no matter where we are or what we are doing. He never leaves us (Ps. 139:7).
- He will search our hearts and show us what it is we need to change (Ps. 7:9; Prov. 20:27; Rom. 8:27; 1 Cor. 2:10).
- He will give us the abilities to do things we need to do—even gifts, wisdom, or words to say (Ex. 31:3; Deut. 34:9; Judg. 14:6; 2 Sam. 23:2; Mark 13:11).
- He will lead us and guide us (1 Kings 18:12; 1 Chron. 28:12; Neh. 9:20; Ps. 143:10; John 16:13; Acts 13:4; 16:6).
- He will show us truth and teach us (John 14:26; 15:26; 16:13; 1 Cor. 2:13; 1 John 2:27).
- He will help us to live the life we need (Rom. 7:6; 8:2, 5–6, 9–11, 13, 26).
- He will fill us and control us (Rom. 8:6; Eph. 5:18).

- He will correct us and convict us (Ps. 139:23–24; John 16:8; Rom. 9:1; 1 Cor. 4:4; Phil. 3:15).
- He will change us (2 Cor. 3:18; Gal. 5:16–25).

This is a lot to expect, but God promises that all these things are available, and that if we ask him for the Spirit, he will come (Luke 11:9–13).

Most of the problems people have in understanding the Holy Spirit come when they are asking for a particular experience of him, or a particular gift (or they are not asking for him at all). If we could get rid of our preconceptions of how or what he is going to do, and ask him to come for the need we have, much of the confusion would go away.

The best way to think about the Holy Spirit and growth is to think about a moment-by-moment relationship of dependency on him. We depend on him to guide us, lead us, talk to us, reveal truth to us, empower us to do what we can't do, give us gifts to be able to give to others what they need, and many other things. But all this happens in an "abiding" sort of way. We yield to him and follow. We open up our hearts and beings to be "filled" with him. We ask him to invade all that we are and to work in us. In a sense, we give ourselves to him as we live out the life of growth.

Therefore, life in the Spirit means that we do not "do growth" without him. It also means that he does not do growth without us. He is at work within us, but there is still an "us." Paul said, "I have been crucified with Christ and I no longer live, but Christ lives in me. The life I now live in the body, I live by faith in the Son of God, who loved me and gave himself for me" (Gal. 2:20).

The old way of trying to "do it right" by ourselves is over (vv. 16, 19). Now we live a life of faith with him inside us. *But we are still the ones who have to live this life and be accountable for it.* As Paul said, "The life I now live in the body, I live by faith." So, as I go through the process of growth, each step I take is a faith step, depending on the Spirit to live it out with me. I live this life as he lives in me.

Practical, Spirit-Filled Living

Just because Spirit-filled living is a mystery doesn't mean we can't do it. Take Julie, for example. Julie had been struggling with eating for several months as her life had gotten more and more stressful. She had prayed about it and confessed her overeating again and again. She felt bad about herself and was getting discouraged. Then she read a piece on how the Holy Spirit could empower her to do what was difficult. So she decided to put that to the test.

Julie's two most difficult tasks were turning from food and bringing people into her struggle. She had been reading about how breaking patterns of behavior had to do with confessing to God and to others and also finding out the root causes driving the behavior. One night she found herself at home alone and wanting to eat ice cream that she knew she did not need. She had just finished a healthy dinner an hour or so before.

She remembered what her growth partners had told her. When you feel tempted, ask God to empower you through his Spirit to do two things: *to turn from what is destructive and to turn to what is good, the things he says to do.* So, in her craving she stopped and asked the Holy Spirit to help her. She prayed for his strength. She sat there with him, and then she asked him to show her what she was feeling. When she did not eat, her feelings of loneliness and stress became clearer to her; then she asked him to help her open up to someone. The name of a friend came to mind. She called the friend, who helped her move past the struggle.

This was a whole new world for Julie. For the first time she didn't have to fight the battle alone. She learned to depend on the Spirit's strength to do what she needed to do, and she yielded to the answers he provided. She also depended on him for help through the support he provided in her friend. *She was both dependent and active.*

The Bible teaches we are to do our part by faith and the Spirit will do his part by his power. It is a real life and a practical life. It is not the life of summoning up willpower and strength we do not possess. Life in the Spirit is one of faith and action. We believe that he will empower and lead us into truth, and then we yield, trust, and step out.

Yielding

Often in the growth process we do not want to do what we know we should do. This is where the "control" of the Spirit comes into play. We must submit to what the Spirit is telling us to do and allow him to have the reins of control moment by moment (Eph. 5:18; Rom. 8:6).

The Holy Spirit brings to mind things God has said, shows us a way out, gives us answers, gives us things to say, and pushes us to take a risk. But when he nudges or reminds, *our job is to yield our will to him and allow him to have control*. In that way, he takes us where we need to go, and we have taken another step of change.

Sometimes we might not even know what that next step is. That's when we can ask God to show us.

"Show Me"

"I don't know why I feel this way," David replied when I asked him what had triggered his depression. "It just hit me. I don't have a clue."

"Let's think about it," I said, knowing that when we talk honestly, more truth usually emerges. We talked, and talked some more, but nothing emerged. Then I felt that urge to pray from the Spirit. So I said, "Let's ask

God to show us through his Spirit what is happening."
And we did.

As we began to talk again, David's face quivered, and
he began to shake. Some powerful emotions came to the
surface as he realized what had triggered his depression.
The day before he'd had a conversation with someone
who had attended a funeral. This conversation had put
him in touch with his feelings over the loss of his mother
at a young age. His depression made total, rational sense.
We, in our limited awareness and knowledge, could not
find the reason, but the Holy Spirit could.

One of the main ministries of the Holy Spirit is that
he leads us to truth—the truth of God and Jesus, the illu-
minating truth of God's Word, the truth about people
through supernatural knowledge, and the truth of situations through wisdom and prophecy. This is what he does.
In fact, he is called "the Spirit of truth" (John 14:17; 16:13).

The Spirit also knows the truth of our own lives
and souls, and he knows what needs to change and be
revealed. I suggest that you ask the Holy Spirit specifically to show you what he wants to reveal to you about
your growth, your soul, issues in your life, and so on.

Ask the Spirit to show you the truth about you as a
person, and also about his answers and God's ways. Truth
is healing, and we need as much of it from him as he will
give. And that is usually as much as we are ready or able
to receive.

Where He Leads, Follow

It has been said that spiritual and emotional growth is a path further and further into reality. I always try to remind people that as painful as it may be, *truth is always your friend.* No matter how difficult it is to swallow, truth is reality, and that is where ultimate safety, growth, and God are. We need to know the truth.

Sometimes the truth leads us to what is hurting us, as with my client David above. Sometimes it leads us to what we need to change. At other times it leads us to what we need to do next in a relationship. At still other times it leads us to what our weaknesses or limitations are, such as what we are *not* ready to deal with.

The flip side to the Spirit's work in this area is that when he leads us to truth, we need to follow.

The Holy Spirit talks to us all in different ways, as everyone's relationship with God is personal. But even though he does it differently with everyone, he does it. He talks to us about our lives and about things we need to change. For me it usually happens in a few ways.

The most common way is when something stays in my mind without my trying to think about it. I have recognized the difference between my own obsessive worry about things and the Spirit's gently "camping out" in my brain. He just sits there constantly with an issue until I deal with it.

Another way is that the Spirit will bring up an issue

from the outside. I will hear the same issue talked about in different contexts, from a sermon to a passage of Scripture, a friend telling me, a book, a radio or TV show, and so on—to the point where I cannot deny he is talking to me.

Then there is the one-time, immediate quickening of my own spirit when I hear or read or see something. The other day, as I was reading some contracts for one of my business deals, I felt my spirit jump inside. I was convicted that the way this relationship was structured was not fair; it was too much in my favor. It is not something I would have come up with, as I had negotiated for my position. But when I read the material, I felt he was speaking to me. It was immediate, and it was strong.

I don't know how you hear the Spirit. Probably you hear him in some similar ways and some different ways as well. If you are a parent, you communicate differently with each of your children, because they hear and learn differently. But our message should always be one of truth. And this is how I think the Holy Spirit operates. He talks to us all in different ways, but always with the truth we need to hear for the moment. Even though it may seem to be "bad news" at the time, it is always good news for the long haul. So listen for how he speaks to you.

One thing is sure: The Holy Spirit can't lead past where he is leading if we don't take that first step of following him into the truth he is showing us. If he shows me an issue, I have to take the steps to deal with it. That is keeping "in step with the Spirit" (Gal. 5:25). It is a relationship we follow step by step.

The best illustration I know of this step-by-step relationship is one I told a man the other day who was thinking of going into the ministry. He was feeling very clearly that God was leading him to drop out of business and attend Bible school, but he did not know what God wanted him to do later, so he did not know what courses to take.

I told him, basically, "Welcome to following God." That is how he usually works. It is like wearing one of those miners' hats with the light on it, I said. You look down and only see enough light to take the very next step. As you take that one, the next one becomes clear, and so on. God rarely shows us the whole picture at once.

We have to "keep in step" with an active following. It is our job to be obedient and follow the little truth he gives us.

Jesus said God is looking for people to worship him in Spirit and in truth. In our limited capacities to know ourselves and to see external reality, we must be dependent on the Spirit of truth to show us those realities. In that way, in the path of truth that he provides, growth happens.

It's Not Just "Let Go and Let God"

When you preach the work of the Holy Spirit in people's lives, there is a danger. Some want to bail out of their responsibility, and they want to "let go and let God." No. We don't just give it all to him. We must "work out our salvation," but we also have to be asking him to help us to do all of it. *It is both, not one or the other.*

Humans tend to be unable to hold opposite ideas in dynamic tension. But this is a tension we will always need to hold: God has a part, and we have a part. Beware of dichotomizing between your tasks and God's.

Supernatural Healing

In addition to the moment-by-moment work and dependency on the Holy Spirit, we can ask him to heal. I strongly believe we can ask God to heal our own souls and to break other kinds of bondage in people's souls.

Throughout the Bible, God is spoken of as healer and deliverer. Sometimes he heals instantly and miraculously. But in the emotional arena with issues like depression, anxiety, and overeating, when people are prayed for, we often see that God begins to heal them by helping them work out their issues. The depressed person, for example, finds the strength and courage to come out of isolation.

The bottom line is that we are to pray for people's healing. I love it when anyone I am working with has a regular prayer group or team praying specifically for the healing of the issues we are dealing with.

Ask God to give you the gifts you need for the moment when you are praying for someone. He may give you supernatural wisdom or knowledge, for example. He may visit you with a gift or manifestation of his Spirit for that person. He may show the person or you what issue should be addressed. Or he may just work a direct miracle—we never know. What we do know is that the "prayer of a righteous person is powerful and effective" (James 5:16). It is as important a part of growth as anything else.

So whether you are growing yourself or are in the process of helping others, make prayer a part of what is happening. Prayer must be in the picture for you to have a complete picture of growth that includes God and his Holy Spirit.

Ask and trust. He will show up, just as he promised.

PART III

Finding The Best Environment

CHAPTER 6

God's Plan A:
PEOPLE

During my own "hitting bottom" experience, I (Henry) went to dinner with a Christian friend. I told him how depressed I had been and how much I felt God had let me down. I had asked God to help me, and I wasn't feeling any better.

My friend listened supportively and gave me Bill's phone number. It turned out that Bill was a student at a seminary. He and his wife, Julie, had a lot of experience ministering to college students.

I went to meet them, and we hit it off. They wanted to know about me and my newfound faith. I told them all about my hand injury, my struggles with trying to play golf in pain for two years, and my decision to give it all up. Then I talked to them about how I had looked around for what I wanted to do and really hadn't gotten anywhere.

To tell you all that happened would be a long story. The short version is that this couple literally took me in. They decided they wanted to "disciple" me—a concept I had never heard of. And since I had nothing else on the horizon, I thought, *Why not?* I decided to take a semester off from school, think about life, live with Bill and Julie, and "get discipled."

I learned a lot about God. Bill gave me access to all his books and took me to his classes. He showed me where the seminary library was, and I fell in love with studying theology. He taught me about doctrine and how to interpret the Bible, and he tried to answer whatever questions I had.

While Bill taught me about God, Julie talked to me about my life. As I opened up, I found there was a lot inside of me I had never thought about. The emptiness I had been feeling was not emptiness at all, but sadness and hurt. I knew I was sad about the loss of my dream to play professional golf, but I got in touch with other losses and hurts as well. Julie had been going through counseling materials that walked one through an "inventory" of the soul, and as we worked through those materials together, I found I had not only hurts, but forgiveness issues. Great loads were lifted off my shoulders as I went through this process.

At the same time, Bill and Julie encouraged me to join a small group that examined my life. The members of this group taught me that I was "emotionally detached" and did not let people get close to me. They showed me I knew very little about love and most of my life had been based on performance and accomplishment, not "abiding intimacy." They challenged all of my relational patterns. At first I felt bad and guilt-ridden when confronted, but later I learned the freedom that comes with being confronted in love. I found out people could discipline me and, at the same time, be for me and not against me.

Another thing happened. Bill and Julie and others saw something in me I had not seen. They said I had a particular gift for understanding the Bible as it relates to counseling issues, and I had the gift of insight into those matters. For my part, I was feeling an increasing desire to study the Bible and counseling. These two paths, the external one and the internal one, merged, and before long I knew God was calling me to go into the field of Christian counseling.

God Uses People Too

One day, some time later—and after getting counseling myself—I realized my depression and my feelings of emptiness were gone. I actually felt good about life and about me. Yet I was both happy and disappointed. God had changed my life, but God had not healed me when I had sought healing. He had not supernaturally "zapped" me.

God's supernatural zapping seemed like Plan A to

me. As I talked about this disappointment, people told me the same thing over and over again: "But God uses people too." I hated hearing that phrase. I had wanted God to touch my depression instantaneously and heal me. Instead, he used people to help me. I came to call this God's Plan B.

Then one day, I made a discovery in Scripture that changed my way of viewing Plan B: "From him the whole body, joined and held together by every supporting ligament, *grows and builds itself up in love, as each part does its work*" (Eph. 4:16, emphasis added).

I read the verse again. Not only was it true that "God uses people too," but this was not Plan B at all! In fact, people helping people was Plan A! The Bible said so. Not only that, but it was not *just people doing it. It was God himself!* God was working directly through people when they were helping me.

This might seem like a nuance, but for me the idea was life-changing. It helped me realize that God was not far off and uninvolved, just delegating things to people. He *wore* people as his uniforms. He came to live inside people and then lived out his wishes and will through them in a mystery called the Body of Christ. Jesus was with me all along by being *in* all of those who were helping me:

> Each of you should use whatever gift you have received to serve others, *as faithful stewards of God's grace in its various forms*. If anyone speaks,

they should do so as one who *speaks the very words of God*. If anyone serves, they should do so with the *strength God provides*, so that so all things God may be praised through Jesus Christ (1 Peter 4:10–11, emphasis added).

I was waiting for God to speak to me directly; he was speaking to me through his people. I was waiting for God to give me direction in life; he was the strength behind the direction people were giving me. I was waiting for him to heal my depression; God himself was healing my depression through my friends Bill and Julie and others.

When I went to graduate school and studied theology, I discovered that this is the doctrine of the church. This doctrine holds that the church, with its indwelling Spirit, is the real physical presence of Christ on earth today. Where two or more are gathered together, he is present (Matt. 18:20). He is inside each believer. He lives in us, and wherever we are, he is. What an incredible reality!

The Role The Body Plays in Growth

Several years later, this reality has become one of the foundational understandings of everything John and I do as professionals. So, as we talk about all the different aspects of how people grow, we want to emphasize loudly the role of the Body. Years of research and experience back up this biblical reality: *You must have relationship to grow.*

As Paul told the Ephesians, to grow up in Christ includes the Body doing its work with each other (Eph. 4:15–16). If you become aware of an area of life in which a person needs something from God, think of other people as part of the solution. Look at the Body resources available to meet that person's needs.

Let's look briefly at some of the roles the Body plays.

Connection

People connected to other people thrive and grow, and those not connected wither and die. It is a medical fact, for example, that from infancy to old age, health depends on the amount of social connection people have.

At the emotional level, connection is the sustaining factor for the psyche, the heart, and the spirit. Virtually every emotional and psychological problem, from addictions to depression, has alienation or emotional isolation at its core or close to it. Recovery from these problems always involves helping people to get more connected to each other at deeper and healthier levels than they are.

The clear teaching of the New Testament is that the Body of Christ is to be people deeply connected, supporting each other and filling each other's hearts.

Virtually every day we receive calls or letters from people who tell their stories of victory over some area of life as a result of getting plugged into a group and working on their issues.

As letter-writer Sandy said, "For years I have struggled with depression and an inability to make relationships work. I prayed, read my Bible, and tried all the things I thought I was supposed to do. Then my church started this group. I could not believe what happened in my life as I began to share openly with other people. I felt connected, and things are so different now. I feel like I am connected to God again."

This connection also impacts people who are in recovery from addiction or compulsive behavior. Hardly anyone completely recovers from an addiction without a support system. Some stop their addictive or compulsive behaviors, but their relational patterns do not change, and most times they relapse if they do not do group work. The reason is complex, but part of it is the alienation driving the addiction itself.

As people are cut off from others and their souls are starved for connectedness, the need for love turns into an insatiable hunger for something. It can be a substance, sex, food, shopping, or gambling, but these never satisfy, because the real need is for connectedness to God and others, and to God through others. When people receive that, the power of addiction is broken.

Discipline and Structure

Self-discipline is always a fruit of "other discipline." Some people get disciplined by other people early in life and then internalize it into their character. Other people don't get disciplined early in life, and they don't ever have self-discipline until they get it from others and internalize it for themselves. It's not rocket science; it's the way God designed us to grow. Others discipline us, and then we can do it for ourselves.

God's Plan A, his "being there," operates when his Body comes together to help someone achieve control over his or her life. Many times in the Bible (as in Matthew 18:15–16; Galatians 6:1–2; Titus 3:10), we are told that we get discipline, structure, and correction from other people whom God gives us, and we are in trouble if we do not: "Mockers resent correction, so they avoid the wise" (Prov. 15:12). So, as you try to grow in self-control over some area of life, consider the constant role of discipline. And if you are helping others grow, make sure that the role of "other discipline" is somewhere in the mix, or growth will stagnate. Whether individually or in groups, we need the discipline, structure, and correction others provide.

Accountability

Accountability is very important, and the Bible tells us over and over again to build it into our lives. But here is the caution: *Accountability is not a cure for lack of self-control.* All it does is "count." It is like the temperature gauge on a car; it can tell you the engine has problems, but it can't fix it. Just as a car must go to a mechanic to get fixed, so the person must get further help past the diagnosis of an accountability group. Accountability is only a monitoring system.

I have been part of the disciplinary process for many spiritual leaders, and I always require them to have an accountability partner or group, *not as the agent of change,* but to make sure they are going to the agents of change. If it is an addiction, are they going to their meetings? Are they going to counseling? Are they doing the spiritual disciplines? The key here is that there is more to the process than accountability. It is necessary but not sufficient.

Grace and Forgiveness

To experience God's grace, our hearts have to be connected to it. We can certainly connect to God "vertically" through prayer, but to feel his grace completely, we have to open our hearts to the full expression of it "horizontally" through other people. Those who only study the "facts" of the grace of God and do not experience other people loving them, as Peter directs us, will fall short in their realization of that grace.

Many people fellowship with others, but they share so little as they fellowship that nothing happens at the heart level. As Paul told the Corinthians, "We have spoken freely to you, Corinthians, and opened wide our hearts to

you. . . . As a fair exchange—I speak as to my children—
open wide your hearts also" (2 Cor. 6:11, 13, emphasis
added). For growth to occur, it must include *experiences*
where hearts are open with each other.

This is one of the meanings behind James 5:16, which
says, "Confess your sins to each other and pray for each
other so that you may be healed." Many Christians do the
vertical confession of 1 John 1:9, where they confess to
God, but not to others. So they "know" they are forgiven
and loved in their head; they just don't "know" it in their
heart. We are made to experience both.

Years ago we treated a pastor for a sexual addiction.
He had confessed and prayed to God over and over again,
but he had not been able to get out of his addictive cycle.
Finally his sense of failure and depression was so great
that he checked himself into our hospital and joined a
group I was leading.

One morning I arrived for a group session, and a nurse
told me that Joe was not going to attend that day—he said
he didn't feel like it. What was really happening, however,
was that the night before, Joe had had a "slip up." He felt
so guilty he did not want to come to the group.

I went to his room and talked him into coming.

As members in the group began sharing, someone
asked Joe if he was okay. He said yes, but we didn't believe
him. This particular morning, I did not let him off the
hook. I prodded him to share with the group. He finally
agreed.

Joe recounted years of sexual acting out and his fears, when he was preaching, that someone would recognize him from the night before. His life was a duplicitous nightmare. He told about how depressed and alienated he felt and, most of all, about his inability to stop.

Then something happened. As Joe was looking at the floor, telling his story, I looked around the room and noticed something: all the members of the group had tears in their eyes; they ached for him. I could feel the compassion and grace in the room. But Joe was not at all connected to the grace available to him.

"Joe," I said, "I want you to look up at the group."

"No," he said. "I can't."

"Yes, you can," I said. "Look up."

Finally, with a struggle, he looked up at the other members. As he looked around the room, he saw the same teary, compassionate eyes I had seen. He saw the gentle smiles. He saw the acceptance. In short, for the first time he saw grace.

He broke. It was like a reed snapping. He fell forward and sobbed like a little child as he experienced grace in the depths of his soul. At that moment his addiction was broken.

Until then, his experience of grace had only been propositional. He had not experienced grace "in the flesh," as the New Testament talks about it. But when the Body did its work, healing occurred.

The point here is that grace can be available to us, but we might not be available to grace. Grace must be experienced to be known. Fellowship on Sunday or at a potluck or a Bible study is great, but fellowship with the depths of the heart is what heals.

Support and Strengthening

When we support something, we hold it up. Throughout the growth process, we will face tasks and realities past our strength and abilities, so we need others to support us. As Paul says, "We urge you, brothers and sisters, . . . encourage the disheartened, help the weak, be patient with everyone" (1 Thess. 5:14). And in another place, "Carry each other's burdens, and in this way you will fulfill the law of Christ" (Gal. 6:2). Support enables people to go through grief, trials, growth, and a whole host of other difficult times.

Recently I was having lunch with a friend I had not seen for years. I asked her about her children, and she proudly told me all about them, and then said, "We lost one."

"What happened?" I asked.

"Well, our four-month-old died of SIDS [sudden infant death syndrome]. He just did not wake up one day."

My breath was taken away, and my heart sank. My own daughter was about that age at the time. I could not imagine how a parent could go through something like that. But here my friend was, a few years down the road, and talking about all God was doing in her life and how blessed she felt. I was really touched by her heart, so I asked her the obvious. "How did you make it through?"

Her answer came immediately and with deep conviction: "The Body," she said. She paused, and then repeated it. "The Body."

She went on to tell me how their friends and the church community had come around them and had been there for them through the experience, holding them up when they were unable to hold themselves up and unable to take the next step.

How could a parent go through the death of a child and come out as she did? How was that possible? Only through the Body. For this is what the physical body does: it sends healing to the injured part of the body. If you have a wounded arm, for example, the body sends antibodies, fresh, oxygenated blood, white cells, anti-inflammatory agents, and so on to that limb. And they do their healing work.

That was what had happened with my friend and her husband. There *is* no way to go through that alone. Many people, however, find themselves cut off from the church and the healing and protective functions it provides. In their isolation—or at least the isolated growth plan they are using—they are easy prey for the gates of hell to overpower them. But, as Jesus said, hell can throw whatever it wants toward us, even death, but his church, the Body, can withstand it all (Matt. 16:18). There is nothing that can prevail against his church.

This is the way God designed it. This is Plan A.

I don't know if my friend fully understood the depth of theology she communicated when she said that the Body is what got her through. But the Bible does understand it. It commands it.

Confronting, Containing Sin, Administering Truth

Part of the role of the Body is to step in and "contain" the effects of sin in someone's life. The Body is sometimes an "antibody"; its role is to fight infection. In Matthew 18:20, we see that two or more together can stop the destructive sin process through Body discipline. As Paul puts it, "Brothers and sisters, if someone is caught in a sin, you who live by the Spirit should restore that person gently" (Gal. 6:1). It is the role of the Body to intervene and save people from the destruction they find themselves in.

But the key is how it is done. Remember, this is the Body of Christ. The way Jesus would do it is, as the verse says, in a spirit of gentleness. He said to the woman caught in adultery, "I do not condemn you, either. Go. From now on sin no more" (John 8:11 NASB). If it is truly an act of the Body, then it will be as if Jesus were there in the flesh, for that is what the Body is. So, when you confront, make sure you are doing it his way, speaking the very words of God (1 Peter 4:11).

Modeling

One day, in a group I was leading, a woman confronted another woman about something the other woman had done. When she spoke of the problem, speaking the truth in love, the other woman responded, owned her behavior, and they reconciled.

As I was listening, I noticed a new member of the group staring at them with a dumbfounded look on her face. Finally I asked the new member what was going on.

"I have never seen that before," she said.

"Seen what?" I asked.

"Well, she was mad at her and told her. And then they didn't get into a big fight. They just talked about it and now it is okay."

The way the first woman had brought up the problem, and the way the second woman responded, was different from anything our new member had ever seen. The new member talked about feeling a strange sense of hope— hope that her own relationships in the future did not have to be the way they had been in the past.

The modeling we experience has a lasting effect upon us, for good or for ill. This is one reason the Bible emphasizes the confession of not only the sins of the people, but also the sins of the fathers (Neh. 9:2). We have to see the wrong modeling we are following in order to renounce it. The goal is to replace the poor modeling with the modeling of people who "imitate Christ," the ones in his Body who show us how he would do it. As Paul said, we imitate those who imitate him (1 Thess. 1:6–7). His Body carries on his walk upon the earth, and others learn it.

Discipleship

It is one thing to sit in a church and receive teaching about the faith, but it is another thing to be taught in a one-on-one relationship. In this context, questions can be asked. Sin can be confessed, and accountability and encouragement offered.

In many circles of self-help spirituality, discipleship and mentoring are lost arts. But we encourage these as a function of the Body for everyone, in two directions. One is to be "under" a spiritual mentor or discipler's care, and to be accountable to that process. The other is to be offering that to someone else who is a little younger or less mature in the faith. Both are important, and both are a developmental role that the Body should play in every life.

A Complete Makeover

The theology of redemption is not one of rehabilitation. It is not as if God comes to us and says, "You look like a good candidate for a 'fixer-upper.' Let's take you where you are and clean you up a little, and then you will be ready for my kingdom and for life." This is not what the Bible teaches at all.

The theology of redemption is one of total destruction, of starting all over again, *at birth*. We are not to be "improved"; we are to be crucified and *born again*. So we need to enter an entire developmental process. John speaks of us as "children" who are learning, whether young or old (1 John 2:12–14). Peter uses the term "newborn babies" (1 Peter 2:2). Hebrews refers to "infants" (5:13). The spiritual developmental path is one of reconciling the creation to the way it was supposed to be.

None of us has made it to adulthood "complete," for we all came from a dysfunctional family: *the human race*. So we have to go through a rebirth and a re-growing up, this time in a new family, God's family. In that family we are to get all the things we missed out on the first time—nurturance, modeling, truth, love, accountability, development of talents—to give us what we need to grow up to maturity and completeness.

God's pattern has always been about life giving life. As he breathed life into mankind, and as that life is passed on by mankind from one person to another, so is spiritual and personal growth. It is produced in one and passed on to another.

Hebrews 10:24 tells us, "Let us consider how we may spur one another on toward love and good deeds." Make sure you are in a Body that is growing you up, and make sure you are designing those experiences for the ones you shepherd. If you do that, you are growing in the way God designed. You are doing it according to Plan A.

CHAPTER 7

How The Richness of Truth
DEEPENS
GROWTH

(John) recently had an encounter with truth that helped me grow. Before I left for work in the morning, my wife told me, "You're sort of distant and preoccupied," and she wanted to know what was wrong. I told her everything was fine. At work, a client mentioned I didn't seem to be emotionally present in the session. I told him it was probably only his perception. A friend at lunch said, "You're here, but you're not here." I told him I was as here as I had ever been. By that time I was getting irritated at the annoying people in my life.

That evening, while I was reading my Bible, I came across 2 Corinthians 6:12: "We are not withholding our affection from you, but you are withholding yours from us." As I meditated on the verse, I realized I had been bombarded with the same truth from several different sources. I also realized I had been preoccupied with a difficult business problem lately, and I had indeed gone inside myself and lost contact with others in my life. It was humbling to see how many different people God used to tell me the truth before I got the message. At the same time, I felt grateful he had not given up on me and had kept sending emissaries until I woke up.

Although we don't always receive it graciously, truth is one of God's essential tools for growing us up. As we will see in this chapter, he gives us many types of needed truth from different sources.

The Many Facets of Truth

The Bible uses the word *truth* to describe different aspects of reality as well as what is true in general (1 Tim. 2:7). The first reality is that of God himself. God is called "the God of truth" (Ps. 31:5 NASB). Jesus calls himself the way, the truth, and the life (John 14:6). The Holy Spirit is also called the truth (1 John 5:6). This illustrates the deeply personal and relational nature of truth. It is much more than a set of facts and rules. Truth lives and breathes in the essence of God.

Since truth is part of God's nature and since we are made in his image, truth is a deep part of our hearts as well. We not only are to know truth, we are to experience it. For example, when I was preoccupied for a whole day, I had an emotional as well as an intellectual grasp of what God was telling me. This is the nature of truth.

The Scriptures also refer to themselves as a whole as the truth. For example, the Bible uses the phrase "the word of truth" to describe itself (2 Tim. 2:15). Jesus said that God's Word is truth (John 17:17). When we read the Bible, we expose ourselves to God's complete guide on the necessary truths of life and growth. What's more, the Bible does not stop with teaching *about* the truths of growth. It is actively involved *in* growth, actively "teaching, rebuking, correcting and training [us] in righteousness, so that the servant of God may be thoroughly equipped for every good work" (2 Tim. 3:16–17).

Also, the Bible uses the word to refer to the specific body of facts regarding Jesus' atoning death for us, which reconciles us to God. This is the gospel, the most important truth of life: "the message of truth, the gospel of your salvation" (Eph. 1:13 NASB).

We can find truth in many places. God uses them all to help us grow in him:

- His Spirit and presence (1 John 5:6)
- The Bible (2 Tim. 3:16)
- People (Prov. 15:31)
- Our conscience (1 Tim. 1:19)
- Circumstances (1 Cor. 10:1–6)

The Kinds of Truth We Need for Growth

As people have different needs, issues, and struggles, truth plays several roles in how it is applied to our lives. Here are some of the principal ways.

Illumination. We need insight and wisdom for our inner lives. A dark part of our lives may need to be exposed and matured. Or we may be ignorant of an issue that needs to be looked at. Illumination is an emotionally corrective experience, when a person has a flash of insight on what is driving a problem.

For example, a friend of mine who was struggling to connect emotionally with his children began exploring his own childhood and discovered, to his surprise, very similar problems with himself and his dad. He felt that a light shone on his entire inner world. He received great help from the truth that God is a father to the fatherless (Ps. 68:5), and ultimately he was able to give to his kids what he had newly received.

Comfort. Comfort is the emotional supply we receive from God and others and then pass on to those who need it to bear the pains of life.

I once saw a woman in a growth group provide healing comfort to a man in three words. He was talking about his job frustrations and protesting his treatment by others, and he was not going to put up with it anymore. The woman listened for a while and then said, "You've been hurt." The man stopped ranting and was silent for a few seconds. Then he began to cry, as her comfort helped him safely move away from rage into the sadness and loss he truly felt. Although we don't naturally associate truth with comfort, it does much to soothe us.

Clarification. We need to understand which of our struggles are our fault, which are the result of someone else's sin, and which are the result of living in a broken world. We need to clarify what is our problem in a relationship and what is not. This is where the truth comes in.

Guidance. Often we stumble through life like little children in the darkness, not knowing how to operate in relationships, in work, or in faith, or even how to guard our hearts. For many people the adult years are very painful, as they feel lost and unsure of their steps. God provides many truths to make our paths straight (Ps. 119:105).

Some of these guiding truths are general principles that apply to all universally, such as the law of empathy for others (Luke 6:31) or the principle of seeking God's kingdom first (Matt. 6:33). In other cases, God provides individual and specific guidance, such as a nudging of the Spirit, a Scripture passage that applies to our situation, or the advice of a trusted friend. None of us are lone rangers, and guiding truths are welcome allies in times of indecision.

Correction. People also need to be confronted with truth when they stray from God's path of righteousness. It is sad but true that we always need to be receptive to correction, as we will see in chapter 10.

Here is a word of caution: If you are a growth facilitator, remember to help your people be exposed to all these types of truth. Some systems of thought only use one, especially the correction type, and provide an unbalanced way of growing people up. In fact, correction used improperly can seriously wound people. Use a full menu of truth, according to the character, maturity, and circumstances of the people you are helping.

How WE Should Approach Truth

Our attitude toward truth makes all the difference in the world in terms of its results in our lives. Here are some stances that can best maximize the healing, growing effects of truth.

Love truth. Struggles in learning to love truth are of two types. Some people have been hurt by truth divorced from love, such as those who have had harsh criticism. Or they have been hurt by inconsistent truth, so they never are sure whether the truth is to help them or to punish them. Other people have experienced more permissiveness than truth. From their perspective, truth has little value because it only hinders them from seeing life the way they want to see it.

When people understand that truth can save and

preserve their lives, it is hard not to love it. When you love something, you pursue it and want to be around it. Don't take a passive role with truth: Hunt it down. Hang around honest people. Invite safe people to tell you the truth about yourself. Pray David's prayer: "Send out your light and your truth; let them guide me" (Ps. 43:3 NLT).

Endure the pain of truth. One of the most valuable tasks for anyone in spiritual growth is to learn to tolerate the discomfort of the truth, in light of its great power to help us. Here are some of the painful experiences associated with truth:

- Facing the reality of our failings
- Living life God's way instead of how we would like to live it
- Loving others when we are aware of their imperfections
- Having truthful conversations with people we love
- Holding onto our values when others judge us wrongly
- Learning new ways that are not easy or natural for us in which to conduct our relationships

This is a difficult list. Yet, remember that the fruit of truth is always worth what it costs us. God is with us when we are with the truth (John 3:21).

Recognize how love helps the pain. Truth's pain carries some hopeful realities. The first is a little formula: *The more love we internalize, the more truth we can bear.* Love gives us the support and grace to tolerate difficult realities. Well-loved people can face their souls without becoming deeply discouraged, for they have been rooted and grounded in love (Eph. 3:17).

This formula also means that as we are loved more, we see things more and more clearly. We are able to look deeper into our souls and see brokenness and sins we may not have been able to tolerate before.

Also, as we are more loved, we don't go into bad places when people we trust tell us the truth. A good friend of mine told me one day that I had been pretty unlovable recently. He was very direct, and then, concerned he had wounded me, he asked me how I was feeling about what he had said. I thought a minute and replied, "We're too close. You just can't hurt me." Maybe he could say something that would really injure me, but it would be difficult at this point. We are used to the fact that each of us is "for" the other person. We all need relationships so knit together with love and truth over time that we can take in who they are and what they say without the risk of injury: "Wounds from a friend can be trusted" (Prov. 27:6).

Be sensitive to truth and untruth. The more a person takes a stance toward truthfulness, the more discerning he becomes about truth and untruth. We become more aware when we are not being honest with ourselves, God, or others, and we sense when someone in our life is being untruthful. God designed us to live in reality. As we immerse our lives in this, we see more and more clearly what is and is not true. Darkness and light become more distinct from each other (John 1:5).

I know a woman who had lived her entire life so afraid of conflict she was unable to see faults in other people. She entered the spiritual growth process and committed herself to admitting and seeing reality, no matter how painful it was. Things began to change. First, she became aware of her own self-deception, attempting to make life comfortable for those in her life. After that, she woke up to her husband's financial irresponsibility and deception, which she had never been able to face. In time, her courage, along with her love for him, helped him to get help. It got to the point that when he would slip up and lie about money issues, she could read it in his face, which was good for both of them: "For you were once darkness, but now you are light in the Lord. Live as children of light" (Eph. 5:8).

Learn to live with mystery and the unknown truths. One more aspect to the role of truth in spiritual growth is learning to live with what we do not, and sometimes can never, know. God alone knows all truth, as he alone can bear the weight of it. It is a mercy from him that we don't know everything about ourselves and the world. At the same time, we are a curious race, and we sometimes feel entitled to have all the answers.

This attitude has all sorts of applications in spiritual growth. There are lots of unknowns we must accept, live with, and move on from, such as the reasons people in our lives did the things they did, the reasons we have done everything we've done, why God allowed certain things to happen, and exactly when we will be through with a particular issue.

Some spiritual growth systems give the impression that we can have answers for all questions. The Bible teaches, instead, that we need to make space for not knowing: "Then I saw all that God has done. No one can comprehend what goes on under the sun" (Eccl. 8:17). We indeed need to pray for wisdom, as Solomon did (1 Kings 3:7–9). But we need also to learn to be dependent on a loving God who dispenses the truths that heal us in the seasons when we most need them.

CHAPTER 8

Water from a Deeper Well:
SPIRITUAL
POVERTY

enry and I (John) were meeting with a large
Christian organization, and the topic of small
groups in the church came up. One of the executives of
the organization, who is a friend of mine, asked, "What
difference do you see between groups for people with
problems and groups for normal people?"

Henry and I looked at each other and said, "There is
just one kind of group."

This illustrates a lingering problem in the church's
view of spiritual growth. Just about everyone would agree
that we all need to grow spiritually. But many do not
believe that a major reason to grow is that we are in a
severe state of neediness.

Yet the Bible teaches that all of us are in this state. The parable of the Pharisee and the tax collector (Luke 18:9–14), and Paul's personal anguish over his inability to do the right thing (Rom. 7:15–24), illustrate how much every person needs God's grace and mercy. By our very nature, we are a broken people, with no hope except for God.

Not everyone is aware of his or her neediness. Many people who have a heart for God and growth have the same split idea of who goes in what group as that friend of mine had. They feel disconnected from those with life problems such as depression, addictions, or anxiety. They may feel compassion and concern for those who struggle, but they can't relate to them. They will sometimes wonder why their friend can't just get it together, snap out of it, or trust God more, since these solutions work for them.

However, Jesus described those who are aware of their neediness as "poor in spirit" (Matt. 5:3). The Greek indicates a cringing beggar, absolutely dependent on others for survival. Not a flattering picture of us! You don't see people greeting each other in church with, "Wow, you're such a cringing beggar. I'd like you to mentor me." Yet the kingdom of heaven belongs to those who experience their dependency.

Spiritual poverty is about living in reality. A good way to understand this is to think of spiritual poverty as experiencing our state of incompleteness before God. This can be due to weaknesses, unfulfilled needs, emotional injuries and hurts at the hands of others, and our own immaturities and sins. It has to do with those parts of ourselves that are not what they should be and that we cannot repair in our own strength. When people experience at a deep level their neediness and incompleteness—the way they actually are—they are often overwhelmed. Spiritual poverty is the cure for narcissism, self-righteousness, and a host of other problems. When our eyes are opened to our brokenness, we do not feel better about ourselves; rather, we feel that something is terribly wrong.

Yet Jesus calls this a "blessed" condition because it helps us get closer to God. Our state of incompleteness drives us outside of ourselves to God as the source of healing and hope. When we are comfortably independent, it is easy to avoid our need for God.

We are not saying that everyone with life problems is poor in spirit. Some are in denial. Others blame their problems on other people. Still others believe that, given enough time, they can solve their problems all by themselves. We are saying, however, that those with life problems have more opportunities to recognize their need for God's healing, because the evidence is right there in front of them.

We are also not saying that those who don't experience problems are in denial. There are many believers who love God, have good marriages and relationships, and have reasonably good lives. They aren't hiding anything. But they may lack a sense of their own brokenheartedness because they are not as aware of their neediness as the reality would indicate.

The Richness That Spiritual Poverty Brings

Spiritual poverty helps us grow because it is both practical and spiritual. Being aware of our incompleteness orients us toward God and his ways, where he awaits us with all we need to grow and repair.

Here is how spiritual poverty brings richness to the growth process.

Spiritual poverty is required for a saving faith. No one can become a Christian who does not admit, at some level, her lostness and hopelessness in freeing herself from the prison and penalty of sin (Rom. 3:23). Otherwise, Jesus' death is meaningless and unnecessary. So to come to saving faith, we must be broken. Although we have God dwelling inside us, we all still have unfinished parts that need to become mature and sanctified. This is why the Bible teaches us to continue in the faith walk as we began it (Col. 2:6).

Spiritual poverty produces a hunger for God. Without poverty, there is no motivating hunger. Lukewarmness is the hallmark of someone who has not yet become poor in spirit and therefore is not hungry. Jesus had harsh words for the lukewarm church of Laodicea: "You say, 'I am rich; I have acquired wealth and do not need a thing.' But you do not realize that you are wretched, pitiful, poor, blind and naked" (Rev. 3:17).

Spiritual poverty drives us to find solutions for our neediness and, ultimately, to find God. Those who know they are truly needy are more motivated to look beyond themselves to the Lord. For example, those in need often become humble in spirit, due to the difficulty of their condition. From there, it is a short step to finding God in so many ways: "The humble have seen it and are glad; you who seek God, let your heart revive" (Ps. 69:32 NASB).

I once worked with a Christian couple who fit both these descriptions. The husband, on the one hand, had a drinking problem, a sexual addiction, and a raging temper. He was a mess, but he was hungry. When he understood the gravity of his problems and his spiritual condition, he went through a long, painful period of deep grieving over what he had done to himself, God, and his family. He made amends to all he could. He went to counseling and several support groups a week, and he voraciously read the Bible and all the books on growth he could get his hands on. He was as vulnerable, correctable, and humble as he could be. His growth took a long time, but he is a new man, and he now has a fruitful ministry to others.

His wife, on the other hand, was caring, structured, and responsible, but she wasn't very hungry for spiritual things. She went to church, read her Bible, prayed when she had time, and lived her life in a moral way. But she is pretty much where she was when I first met her. Her only problem back then, in her mind, was a crazy husband. And now she feels that life is better because he is better.

I often tried to talk to her about her own hurts and issues, and she basically shut it all out. Even though she has a good life, she touches no one deeply and lets no one in, including God. Her children are distancing more from her as they grow, because there's nobody inside. She just wasn't hungry.

The more broken we are, however, the more God can grow us up.

Spiritual poverty helps us endure the pain of growth. While spiritual growth is hard work—it means losing your life, including all the old comfortable patterns, to find your life in Christ (Matt. 16:25)—poverty makes it hard to go backward in the process. Once your eyes are opened to your need, it is difficult to live as though you had none. It is as if a door has been opened that can't be shut.

I was counseling a woman who had made a commitment to grow spiritually. During the process she began to feel the lonely, isolated emotions she had had as a little girl when she had needed a grownup mother and didn't have one. These times were painful for her, both relationally and internally. Yet she never wavered in her commitment: "I don't see how I could pretend as if what was wrong is really right anymore," she told me. "So I actually feel blessed to be in this position in my life."

She endured the pain of growth because her spiritual poverty kept her involved in God's ways.

Spiritual poverty keeps us living relationally. Coming to the end of ourselves reduces us to a childlike state of need and helplessness, which Jesus said is good: "Truly I say to you, whoever does not receive the kingdom of God like a child will not enter it at all" (Mark 10:15 NASB). Children by nature are relationally oriented. When they are in trouble or pain, the first thing they do is reach out for a protective, comforting parent. They don't say to themselves, *I'll be strong and ride this one out, or I'll just think positive thoughts.* They ask for help from someone outside themselves.

One of the blessings of spiritual poverty is that it helps restore to us God's design of a relationally based life. We learn to receive comfort, support, and acceptance from him and others, which then strengthens us to continue.

Spiritual poverty helps us enter the deeper life. Our broken-hearted state also provokes us to move beyond spiritual immaturity into a deeper walk of faith. Although we all begin our spiritual lives as babes (1 Peter 2:2), God did not intend for us to stay in that stage of development forever. The deeper walk takes us into many areas—the mystery of God's nature; the wonders of the Bible; the complexities of our own personality and issues; and the intricacies of intimate relationships with others. Once we are on the path to growth, we are called to continue it at new levels.

Spiritual poverty guides us to specific growth areas. Spiritual poverty helps us find the right issues to heal. Physically hungry people are not always hungry for the same things. They may desire meat, vegetables, or fruit. In the same way, spiritually hungry people are not always hungry for the same things. Spiritual poverty can help us find particular areas of need and growth.

How? By making seekers out of us. Seekers tend to look in many directions for answers and help. They pray and ask God for insight and wisdom about their condition. They search the Bible. They ask mature people for counsel. And God promises that, in his timetable, they will find what they are looking for. He loves for us to seek. Jesus said, "Ask and it will be given to you; seek and you will find; knock and the door will be opened to you" (Luke 11:9).

How To Develop Spiritual Poverty

Becoming poor in spirit is one of the most unnatural things we can do—it is the opposite of being victorious and having it together. Yet it is our only hope for spiritual growth.

Actually, our task is more realizing our poverty than becoming poor, as we are already in need whether we know it or not. It is better to seek this quality ourselves than be forced to face it by difficult circumstances. Let's look at some ways that we can develop this internal capacity.

Ask God. Being in touch with your spiritual poverty is a gift from God because it brings forth things he wants to see in you and because it accomplishes his purposes. He will gladly show you where you are weak.

Become an honest person. Do an honest review of your past and present life. Look for patterns of avoiding pain, denying problems, staying away from truthful people, and trying to put a positive spin on negative things in your life. Be honest about tendencies to shy away from need and to move toward pride and self-sufficiency.

Look closely at those negative things you might be avoiding. Seeing the reality of your state can go a long way toward promoting your growth in spiritual poverty. Ask God for the grace and love to help you tolerate what you find inside (Ps. 139:23–24). Here are a few categories of issues:

- **Sins.** Look at selfish, rebellious behaviors and attitudes. Although you have been forgiven for them, they still require confession and repentance. Look especially beyond behaviors into dark motives of the heart: withdrawal of love, vengeance, envy, and blaming.
- **Hurts and losses.** All of us not only have sinned, but

also have been sinned against and injured. Look at significant people in your life who have hurt you. Also, look at failures and losses in life, such as medical, financial, or career losses.

- **Weaknesses.** Identify character flaws that hamper your life, things you do that you can't stop doing. This might include irresponsibility, control, fragility, people-pleasing, and perfectionism.

Try not to be too legalistic with this short list, as there is much interplay between categories. Irresponsibility, for example, can involve both sin and weakness, and it can be influenced by hurt. For growth purposes, however, this list can help you see your need for God.

Read the teachings of the Bible on the topic. Look up terms such as *poor in spirit, needy,* and *brokenhearted,* and learn what the Bible teaches about them. Look at the dynamics of God's relationship with Israel in the Old Testament. When she was complacent or rebellious, he was hard. When she was poor and hurting, he was tender. Study the differences in how Jesus addressed those who were wanting and those (like the Pharisees) who thought they had it together. The Scriptures give overwhelming evidence that spiritual poverty is an essential element of growth.

Get feedback from others. One characteristic of hungry people is that they surround themselves with others to help them with their dependency. For them, the normal

Christian life is one in which people get together, share vulnerabilities, and fill each other up. If you are just entering into a position of poverty, however, ask those you trust if they think you are needy and poor in spirit. The honest ones will understand and will graciously let you know the truth.

Seek a wholehearted experience of brokenness. Poverty of spirit requires more than cognitively admitting we are incomplete and needy. It is an overwhelmingly emotional experience, involving feelings such as dependence, grief, and remorse. Psychologists call this "being integrated," having the heart and head in alliance with each other. Seek this experience in the same way you seek God: "If . . . you seek the LORD your God, you will find him if you seek him with all your heart and with all your soul" (Deut. 4:29).

God reminds us, time and time again, that he likes neediness. Our life experiences might tell us to avoid need. If so, take a faith step and open up your soul to God and safe people. Spiritual poverty is the only way to be filled with what he has for us.

CHAPTER 9

The Warmth of
FORGIVENESS

No matter how many times I read that I'm forgiven, I just don't feel like it," Stephen said. "I know the Bible tells me God accepts me. I just have to believe it more, I guess."

"Do you *disbelieve* him?" I (Henry) asked. "Do you have any reason to doubt God forgives you?"

"No, I believe it. He says so. I just can't feel it," Stephen replied.

"Then, why do you say you need to believe it more? Why do you think it's a 'believing' problem if you already believe it?"

"Because my friends tell me the Bible says the truth will set you free, and if I don't feel free from guilt, then I don't know the truth. That's why I think I need to believe the truth better."

Stephen had been acting out sexually. Every now and

then he would have a "slip" (as he called it) and go to the internet and view pornographic websites. At other times he would have one-night stands and feel horribly guilty later. Even after he had confessed and asked God to forgive him, the guilt would remain for days, and he would be unable to shake it. When he could not get rid of his guilt, he would act out sexually again to find relief. But instead of relief, it would bring more guilt, and the cycle would begin all over again. What he *knew in his head* about forgiveness was different from what he *felt in his soul.*

He is not alone. We see this same cycle in other behaviors, such as overeating. People will overeat and feel guilty, and then to feel better they will overeat again. Then the guilt comes back, because they are traveling in an endless circle.

So how are we to help Stephen? And what do we do when we *are* Stephen, for many of us can identify with not feeling as forgiven as we are? What are the steps, and how do we take them? That is the subject of this chapter. We will look at the causes of guilt, some misconceptions about dealing with it, and how the spiritual growth process can resolve it.

The Source and Resolution of Guilt

Remember our discussion of the Fall in chapter 2. When we fell, we went into a state of separation. Later in the Bible, Paul explains that this separation from God was a state called *death* (Rom. 5:12). It was not cessation of life. Instead, it was separation from Life itself. As a result, we were under the wrath and condemnation of God and his law; we were found guilty in the cosmic court of God. And as the Bible puts it, that law brings about two things: guilt and God's wrath (Rom. 4:15).

But God provided an answer to this problem. Jesus paid the penalty for our sin against God (Rom 6:23), and we were declared "not guilty" (Rom. 3:22). As a result, we are reconnected to God; we now have an unbroken and alive relationship with him. Nothing can come between God's love and us ever again (Rom. 8:33–39).

The verdict is "not guilty." No separation. No anger or wrath. Those who have a relationship with Jesus have no reason to fear condemnation. The New Testament makes this point over and over again (John 3:18; Heb. 10:13–14, 17–23).

We go from guilty to not guilty by believing. This is the theology of guilt in the Christian faith. A "guilty Christian" is an oxymoron.

But Stephen still *feels* guilty. What's his problem?

Two Sides, Two Experiences

The Bible talks about our legal standing before God, about how God feels toward us. How *we* feel in response to how God sees us is the other side of the equation.

Have you ever been in a relationship where someone needed constant reassurance of your love? Your loved one asked you over and over again if you cared, and no matter what you did to show your love, it did not get through. After a while you realized that your reassurances were not all that was needed. She had a problem in her heart. She had a block to feeling love.

It is the same in our relationship with God. Our hearts can condemn us even when God does not (1 John 3:20; 4:18). So we have to ask, "What are the conditions inside of us that prevent us from feeling forgiveness even when we are surely forgiven?" Let's look at some of the answers.

Wrong Teaching

Some Christians have never been taught how forgiven they are when they believe in Jesus. Many have been taught that we are forgiven until we sin again and then we need to be forgiven all over again. Then they struggle with whether or not their confession was good enough.

Our sins truly have been forgiven once and for all, and there is truly "no condemnation." So the first thing we have to make sure of is that people understand: if they are reconnected to God, they are not guilty. Their problem may not be that their emotions are not following their knowledge. They may just not know.

In cases like this, it is crucial that people learn what the Bible really says. Meditating on and memorizing Scripture verses about forgiveness and grace should be a part of their regular diet. They need to be able to answer their internal accusations with God's truth. But all of this assumes that a person is confessing his sin to God and asking for forgiveness. We can only receive God's forgiveness to the degree we are confessing. If confession is taking place, God will cleanse and purify us (1 John 1:9).

Disconnection from Grace

Jake struggled with overwhelming guilt because of his depression. He had been working on his depression for some time, but was not getting well as fast as he thought he should. I would talk to him about giving himself some grace, but he just could not cut himself any slack.

He needed grace before his depression could be resolved. Since he was praying and getting all the grace he could directly from God, I figured Jake needed more grace from God's people, so I put him in a group.

The difference was profound. Those people had the acceptance for him that he did not have for himself, and their grace touched him. He found that as others gave him grace, he could give himself more space to be where he was.

God has mysteriously wired us so that what was once outside of us comes inside. Based on our past relationships, we learn how to accept or reject ourselves. Our relationships and their messages are internalized in our brains. If people reject themselves or some part of themselves, part of the answer is encouraging them to join a supportive, accepting community so they can internalize new ways of feeling toward themselves. James says, "Therefore confess your sins to each other and pray for each other so that you may be healed" (James 5:16). As we do that, we internalize from each other the grace we need.

False Standards

In addition to receiving grace from the group, Jake discovered that his standard of "I should be over this by now" was false. It was easy to criticize himself as long as he compared himself with an unreal standard inside his own head. But when he got into a group, he found that others struggled as well; he was not the only one. He was not defective.

People who grow up with unrealistic standards from their parents, the media, or the culture often have an "ideal" person in their head to which they compare themselves, and the result is relentless guilt or shame. Their perfectionist standard beats them up daily. Jesus, on the other hand, said that we are broken and sick and need a physician. This is the standard the Bible tells us to use. David says God the Father "has compassion on his children . . . for he knows how we are formed, he remembers that we are dust" (Ps. 103:13–14).

God remembers the standard he measures us by. Often we forget. The biblical standard is not people who have never failed; it is people who, when they failed, got reconnected to God and went on in faith. The people listed in the hall of fame in Hebrews 11 were real people with real problems, yet God lists them as models for us to emulate. God has never looked for perfect people, just faithful ones. All of us should be comparing ourselves with this standard, not the one of perfection. Resolving guilt and shame always involves getting people to see themselves as fellow strugglers instead of super humans. As Paul says, we experience nothing that is not in some way common to humankind (1 Cor. 10:13).

When people confess to one another (James 5:16), they find that out. They find out they are not weird and different, but are just like everyone else: fellow sojourners. This cuts down tremendously on guilt. If you are divorcing, get together with other people who have gone or are going through a divorce. If you are an addict, get together with other addicts. Strugglers need to be with strugglers. And in reality, that's all of us.

Weak Conscience

A weak conscience can keep us from feeling forgiven. On face value, when we think of a "weak conscience" we probably think of one that does not work well—it is one too weak to stand up to our impulses. But in the Bible's view, it is just the opposite. A "weak conscience" is one that is *too* strict and is confused on the issues of right and wrong. Sometimes a weak conscience can convict people of things that are not even real issues (1 Cor. 8:7–12).

Usually the weak conscience comes from too strict a

background, wrong teaching, a fear of losing control, or not enough safety for someone to find out what is helpful and real. If people feel guilty for things that are not even issues, they need the safety and grace of an accepting environment—first, to find out what the Bible really teaches, and second, to face their own appetites and impulses. As they gain the strength that comes from maturity and community, they will not need rigid rules to hold them in check. Self-control takes the place of guilt as the gatekeeper of impulses.

Godly Sorrow Versus Worldly Sorrow

Paul distinguishes between two kinds of sorrow: "Godly sorrow brings repentance that leads to salvation and leaves no regret, but worldly sorrow brings death" (2 Cor. 7:10).

The angry, condemning conscience is worldly sorrow at work. It is not based in love and does not bring about lasting change and repentance. It is based on one's own badness. Worldly sorrow is the kind Judas expressed after he betrayed Jesus—he went out and killed himself. Godly sorrow is the kind Peter expressed after he denied Jesus. Heartbroken for the hurt he caused someone he loved, he moved toward the relationship and reconciled.

Whenever we talk in our seminars and on the radio about guilt being hurtful, people become upset. They think you need guilt to keep people in check. "People should feel guilty when they do wrong. It is healthy guilt," they say. But the Bible does not say this. *The Bible says we should not feel guilty, but we should feel sorry. There is a big difference.*

Guilt focuses on me. It focuses on how bad I am, not on what I have done to hurt you. If I am feeling guilty, I am concerned about feeling good again, not about the destructiveness of the problem or the way I may have hurt someone. Guilt is self-directed.

On the other hand, godly sorrow focuses on the offended party. Those who express godly sorrow empathize with how their behavior has affected someone else. This is why the Bible talks about God being "grieved" when believers sin. Instead of our feeling guilty, he wants us to be concerned with how we have hurt him with our sin. Godly sorrow is "other directed."

The difference is astounding. As Paul says, godly sorrow ends up in repentance. When we realize we are hurting someone we love, we change. Love and empathy change us. We treat others as we would want to be treated. Love constrains us. But guilt actually causes sin to increase (Rom. 5:20; 7:5). It does not keep anyone in check. It only makes people rebel more.

This happened to Stephen. The guiltier he felt and the further he put himself under the law, the more his sin would increase. Guilt failed to keep him in check. If he could have gotten in touch with how he hurt the women he was acting out with, this could have changed him. His care for breaking their hearts, splitting their souls, and keeping them from God could have turned him around. Instead, he was too concerned with how "bad" he was.

The bottom line is that guilt is about the law and godly sorrow is about love. The Holy Spirit is always about love. When he convicts us, he is not trying to make us feel "bad and condemned." He is trying to get us to see how we are hurting God, others, or ourselves by our behaviors or attitudes. And if we can see that, love will "cause repentance."

True Guilt and False Guilt

As Christian counseling grew popular during the seventies, counselors noticed that sometimes people felt guilty for no good reason. In an attempt to help them, they coined the term "false guilt." For things that were not really "bad," people should see their guilt as inappropriate, label it "false guilt," and give it up. Great advice: No one should feel bad about things that are not bad.

But the problem was on the other side of the equation. These people also taught that people *should* feel guilty for the bad things they did. They called this "true guilt."

There are behaviors, attitudes, and choices that are wrong. There is no question about that. When we commit an offense, *we are guilty of committing this offense*. But this does not mean that our proper response is to feel guilty and condemned.

The beginning of Romans 8 annihilates our guilt all together, but it does not say we have nothing to worry about. It says we have to worry about how we are living and what we are doing, for we are either producing life or death by how we are living our lives. It has nothing to do with guilt, but with what sin does to us:

> Therefore, brothers and sisters, we have an obligation—but it is not to the flesh . . . If you live according to the flesh, you will die; but if by the Spirit you put to death the misdeeds of the body, you will live. For those who are led by the Spirit of God are the children of God. The Spirit you received does not make you slaves, so that you live in fear again; rather, the Spirit you received brought about your adoption to sonship. And by him we cry, "*Abba*, Father" (Rom. 8:12–15).

Guilt pushers do not like to get rid of guilt, for they fear that if people do not have guilt to stop them, they will do whatever they want. But the Bible is clear: guilt does nothing to help, but getting a picture of what sin is doing to one's life does.

Guilt as an Old Voice

"I just feel mean telling her that," Joyce said.

She was referring to a conversation she had had with

a friend about that friend's marriage. Her friend was not confronting her husband on how he was treating their teenage son. He was going back and forth from ignoring their son's behavior to confronting him angrily, and the problem was getting worse. Joyce was concerned that her friend was sitting back, passively letting her husband hurt their son. So Joyce had told her friend she was being too passive and her son was going to get worse if she did not do something.

"Why do you feel mean?" one of the group members said. "That was a very loving thing to do, and you did it in a nice way. I wish I had a friend like you who would tell me when I'm not doing what I should be doing with my son."

"But I felt horrible after I left her. I felt like I had hurt her feelings."

"Did she act like it?" another member of the group asked. "Did she get mad?"

"No, she said I was right, and she asked me to help her figure out what to say. But I just feel so bad."

"Well, someone's accusing you," another member said, "but it's not her, and it's not us. And it's surely not God. He tells us to do what you did. That was an act of love."

"What do you mean 'someone'?" she asked.

Good question. As Joyce talked, she began to see a pattern. Every time she would be lovingly honest with someone (Eph. 4:25), she would feel bad. She was doing what the Bible told her to do—a good deed. But her honesty had not been seen as good in past relationships.

This is one of the most important dynamics about guilt. Internal ties and old relationships are replayed inside the soul, and people feel the same feelings they felt with those people until they work through those feelings. And usually the guilt has to do with the expression of some aspect of one's personhood, as Joyce experienced. She felt guilt about her truth-telling parts.

Any aspect of ourselves that is disapproved of or attacked in a significant relationship can come under "judgment," and then guilt attacks that part of the soul from the inside. If a parent, for example, belittles a child's need for affection, a punitive voice against that part of the child gets internalized. This is partly how our conscience is formed. Then, until the conscience gets modified, this person will feel guilt whenever he expresses that aspect of himself, even if it is a good part. So, many times people have to express themselves in new, safe relational settings to get the healing and encouragement God provides to restore the soul. A new conscience has to be internalized and developed in new relationships. Again the Body of Christ does its work.

Anger

We saw above how aspects of the self can be paired with guilt messages, and certainly anger is one of those. Some people feel guilty whenever they feel themselves getting angry. But there is another problem with anger.

Anger is a state of protest and fight. It is a problem-solving emotion designed to protect what is good and what is valuable. God wired this emotion into us to be "against" something. We use anger to fight injustice, unrighteousness, evil, and other bad things. But sometimes people have not expressed anger toward bad things that have happened to them because those things have happened in a context in which expressing anger would have been dangerous. So these people deny their anger. The problem is that anger is directional; it has to be aimed at something.

It is supposed to be aimed at injustice or the person who is being unfair. But if this is not possible—for example, in cases of child abuse—people will aim the anger at themselves instead. Abused children feel, "I am bad if this is happening to me."

So sometimes the cure for guilt has nothing to do with helping people feel "forgiven." It has to do with helping them resolve their anger toward whomever or whatever deserves it.

Isolation

One of the most misunderstood aspects of guilt is that guilt is basically about separation from love. As John says, "There is no fear in love. But perfect love drives out fear, because fear has to do with punishment" (1 John 4:18).

If people know they are loved, they are not afraid of their "badness." They feel accepted and safe. Love does that. Love is everything. *In the Bible, the opposite of "bad" is not "good." It is love.*

So if people are feeling bad about themselves, the answer is never to get them to feel better about themselves. The "self-esteem" trip is a dead end. The answer is to have them feel connected to love. If they feel connected and accepted, they do not have to feel good about themselves. In fact, they stop being so concerned about themselves altogether.

One of the most destructive causes of guilt is emotional and spiritual isolation. If you find people who feel bad about themselves, find the isolated part of their heart and give them grace, love, and connection. Reconciliation to love is the answer for guilt of any kind.

The Good News

Jesus said that he did not come into the world to judge or condemn it (John 12:47). If this is true, how on earth did the institution he began, the church, turn into one of the guiltiest places on earth? This is a big problem. The One who came to end guilt has it dished out in his name over and over. Yet as we have seen in this chapter, the Bible teaches there should be no guilt for the Christian. Instead, there should be the freedom of "no condemnation" along with a deep concern for real problems and issues.

So as you work on your guilt or the guilt of others, remember that it is not a problem, but a symptom of being separated from Love. And the solution is always reconciliation to Love. It "never fails" (1 Cor. 13:8).

PART IV

The Way To Growth

CHAPTER 10

The Value of Pruning: DISCIPLINE

The Bible teaches that everyone needs discipline and correction to grow: "My son, do not despise the Lord's discipline, and do not resent his rebuke" (Prov. 3:11).

Let's understand what we are talking about. The Bible has many meanings for the word *discipline*. The idea for our discussion is that discipline in its broadest sense is training for a person to learn self-control in some area of life. The word *discipline* describes both the process and the result. *We become disciplined by being disciplined by God and others.*

Why do we need to be disciplined to learn self-control? Because we are not in control of ourselves. Like children, we go astray, make mistakes, and need parameters. One of the fruits of the Spirit is self-control (Gal. 5:23), and it comes from God over time so that we can run our lives under his rule. And like children, we know when it has borne fruit inside us *when we are not as dependent on the outside structure to stay in control.*

Our need for discipline applies to much more than problems in organization and structure. It applies to every area of life in which we are not operating as we should, from attitudes to relationship conflicts to faith struggles.

Some people fear that discipline means punishment, condemnation, judgment, or even abuse because others may have hurt them in the guise of discipline. But God's view differs greatly from that. One of the Greek words used in the Bible for *discipline* has a meaning that includes "nurture." That is to say, discipline assists in lovingly growing us up. It is driven not by anger or punitiveness, but by caring (Heb. 12:6).

Submitting to discipline is difficult because we must allow something to be done to us, and then we grow from it. This might mean giving someone permission to confront us when we are unloving, or agreeing to be in a group that will tell us the truth about ourselves. A certain loss of control and self-protection is necessary when we want to learn discipline. God never makes growth a process we can fully control. It takes faith.

We also need to take initiative and be active. Paul says it this way: "I strike a blow to my body and make it my slave so that after I have preached to others, I myself will not be disqualified for the prize" (1 Cor. 9:27). *We are an active part in the discipline we allow to happen to us.*

The Ingredients of Discipline

Several aspects to discipline operate in our hearts and aid our spiritual growth. Some are qualities of the person being trained, and some are qualities of the process. When the discipline works as it should, these all add up to much growth.

What the Grower Must Provide

Receptiveness. The more we embrace the necessary pains of growth, the more discipline bears fruit (Heb. 12:11). I have seen people receive the lessons of discipline and grow from them to the point that they made major strides in their sanctification. I have also seen people refuse discipline, and their lives have suffered as a result. King David humbly received God's correction when he went off the path, and his kingdom was established forever. In contrast, the pharaoh of Egypt, a man with a high position, hardened his heart against the discipline of God, and he came to a tragic end.

If you are a growth facilitator, normalize this receptivity in your growth context. Make sure that truth and loving confrontation are integral parts of the process, not exceptions.

Confession. To "confess" is to agree with the truth. When God or others are disciplining us, we need to agree on the issue or problem. When we confess, we are aligning ourselves with the process of growth and repair (James 5:16).

125

When we do not confess, we can negate discipline's good effects. Confession begins the process of repair.

Repentance. When we encounter God's discipline, we need to be willing not only to agree with the truth but to live out the truth—that is, repent. Repentance means that we truly will change what needs to be changed. It is important to note here that this doesn't always mean fixing the problem itself immediately. If that were true, there would be no need for growth. Repentance would simply mean doing only the right things and avoiding all the wrong things—which can't be done, given our immature and sinful condition (Romans 7).

It is better to see repentance as an attitude of turning both from what is not the best and toward the good. This helps us move from death to life.

What the Process Must Provide

A source. Discipline must come from the outside until we develop self-control and maturity. God provides more than one source of discipline.

First, he chastens and corrects us directly. It all started when he had to put his first kids in a permanent time-out from the Garden of Eden (Gen. 3:23–24)! I (John) remember a friend of mine losing a high-paying job during an industry slowdown. This loss was not because of any performance issue on his part. However, it happened during a time when he had been paying more attention to his work than his family and his inner life. He told me later that he believes his job crisis was a signal from God to get his spiritual house in order, which he did.

Second, people are a source of discipline. It is hard to overstate the importance of the Body here. We need caring, honest, perceptive people who will love us enough to correct us when we stray. David had Nathan (2 Sam. 12:1–14); Peter had Paul (Gal. 2:11).

Third, reality is also a source of discipline. God has constructed the universe to operate with certain laws. When we disobey those laws, we feel the pain of the consequences. For example, when we don't listen to the feelings of others, they will disconnect from us. This discomfort alerts us to the task of reaching out to others' hearts.

Empathy from others. Discipline must also be administered with gentleness and care. We can bear consequences when we know that God and others are doing it to correct us, not to punish us.

Stay away from having parental or controlling attitudes toward those who are enduring discipline. Make sure they are treated as adults, with respect and freedom. Remember what it feels like when you are admonished.

Pain. Discipline generally requires pain to be effective. Pain signals a problem to which we should pay attention. God, people, and reality administer that pain in the right dosages for us to see what is going on, and then we correct ourselves.

The kinds and dosages of pain differ according to our need. A person with a receptive heart needs less pain to get the message. Someone who is egocentric or naturally strong-willed may need more.

Remember also that there are other kinds of pain in the world besides the pain of discipline. Losing a loved one, for example, may not be a wakeup call, but merely the sad reality of living in a broken world. People can hurt each other needlessly by always attributing pain to the need for discipline. If you are a growth facilitator, be careful to distinguish between events and patterns. Events do not generally require much discipline; patterns do.

Internalization. Internalization is the process of emotional learning that means a person has made the experience a part of herself. She no longer needs the external structure and pain, because she has taken in the lesson and grown from it.

For example, a woman in a group I led didn't realize that she dominated the conversation and always led the subject back to herself. The group members lovingly let her know how it distanced her from them and how much they wanted to get past it to be close to her. It hurt her to hear it, but she submitted to the process and asked them to remind her when it happened again. They did that faithfully. In time, she would catch herself controlling things verbally before anyone said anything. Then later, she became much more connected with the group, with no hint of the controlling tendencies she once had. She had internalized many experiences of loving discipline from her group.

What Needs Disciplining?

How do we know what to correct and what to let go? This is an important question, since many extremes exist on both sides. Some people function as moral police officers and constantly rebuke others to the point of hurting them. Others ignore the value of discipline and refrain from confronting people. Here are some guidelines for how to think about disciplining.

Problems arising from ignorance. Some people struggle in life or relationships because they are ignorant of the issues. It's not that they resist or deny their issues. Rather, they are more innocent; they don't know there's a problem. For example, I have a friend who has a loud voice. She wasn't aware of it, but I noticed it in public places. When I mention it to her, she talks more softly. She encounters discipline in my reminders to her, but she is humble about accepting feedback.

Problems in lack of structure. Many people find they do not have enough internal structure to confront problems with others, stay focused on goals, make good choices, and think long-term. The discipline process can be extremely helpful, because the structure of the discipline creates what the person lacks.

Think of a child who can't attend to homework for more than a few seconds. You can nag the child all day, and she won't be able to stay on task. But when you design a disciplining structure that provides love, parameters, and appropriate consequences (for example, specific amounts of time required studying, with a loss of playtime if she doesn't stay on task), the child over time is more likely to develop the ability to work steadily.

Character patterns. We need to be aware of, and discipline, disruptive character patterns such as emotional detachment, passivity, controlling others, self-centeredness, irresponsibility, and perfectionism. Some ways we interact with God, others, and the world do not work well. At their core, these are generally long-standing immaturities within us that are often the cause of more external problems: depression, anxiety, marital and dating struggles, financial struggles, substance abuse. When we accept discipline for them, we obtain wisdom on dealing with them and support for resolving them. Ultimately, they mature and are no longer issues.

Erring toward comfort. Be aware, however, that some spiritual growth concerns may need more love than correction. For example, people who are brokenhearted and needy may benefit from reminders of the issues, but what they need more are safety, comfort, and love.

A case in point is a man I knew who struggled with anger. His growth group corrected and corrected him. He tried to respond well, but felt more helpless and guilty each time they corrected him. Finally, his counselor diagnosed an underlying depression that was driving his anger. His depression had to do with deeply sad feelings of loss. When he was comforted in his grief, the depression and anger resolved.

Discipline Busters

Sadly, we all tend to sabotage the growth process. Especially if you are a facilitator, be able to recognize the many ways we turn from God's growth paths, because more than anything, they can render spiritual growth null and void until they are resolved. Here are four.

Denial. Denial is not admitting the truth about a problem. There are two types of denial: One is when we keep something hurtful away from our awareness, such as trauma; the other is when we don't want to admit we have responsibility for something, such as how selfish we can be. The second is much more serious than the first. An example of this might be someone who has a habit of being critical of others, but when people say something about it, responds with "No, I don't do that."

Rationalization. When we rationalize, we make excuses for our problem to avoid being blamed. We may admit the problem exists, but it's not our responsibility. Using the above example, the person might say, "I do criticize you, but it's constructive."

Minimization. To minimize is to lessen the perception of the problem, or dilute it. For example, the person might say, "I really don't criticize you like you think I do. You're being oversensitive."

Blame. Blame takes the responsibility squarely off the shoulders of one and lays it on another. It points the finger anywhere but toward us. For example, "I criticize because you provoke me to do it; you continue to show up late all the time."

At the heart of all of these "discipline busters" is our attempt to remove a bad aspect of ourselves from us. This is called "projection," and it is what Jesus referred to when he warned us to remove the plank from our eye before concentrating on the speck in our brother's eye (Matt. 7:1–5). People project so that they will not have to experience the discomfort of their own weaknesses and sins. These projections divide people and disrupt the growth process. This is why, when you become aware of denial, rationalization, minimization, or blame, you must lovingly but directly confront it.

Case in Point

I am a personal testimony to this chapter! While writing a section of this book, I encountered a problem. Buried with other tasks and projects, I got behind in my writing schedule. Nothing I did helped me catch up. I put time aside, prayed, resolved to do better, and drank coffee late at night, all to no avail.

Finally, I called people in my growth group and asked them to do three things for me. First, I asked them to let me give them a copy of my writing deadlines so they would be aware of when I had to have what parts written. Second, I asked them to call me twice a day to see whether I was on schedule. Third, I asked them to decide what favorite charity they would like me to send money to, as long as it wasn't one of my favorites, so it would sting a little. And it worked. Knowing my friends were on my side and would be in touch with me helped me stay on task.

A friend who heard about this tactic said, "But why didn't you use rewards instead of discipline?"

I told her, "I couldn't take the chance."

The reward of relief came later when I made the deadline anyway.

Conclusion

Discipline provides a structure for growth. If we stay in the correction process "correctly," we will grow, not only in self-control, but in love, faith, and responsibility.

CHAPTER 11

Pulling The Weeds of
SIN AND
TEMPTATION

Back in the 1980s, I (Henry) remember listening to a minister give his opinion on the recovery movement, which was becoming popular in the church. He was angry. People were getting off too lightly, and he was not going to stand for it. I can almost hear his words today: "What's all this stuff about people being 'powerless' over their addiction? This is not what the Bible says! People are free moral agents and responsible for their sin! People choose to sin, and they are responsible for their choices! It's just sin, period."

The minister was obviously upset at hearing people in recovery talk about Step One in the Twelve-Step Process:

"We admitted that we were powerless over alcohol—that our lives had become unmanageable." To him, powerlessness was a cop-out. He thought people needed to admit they were choosing wrong and begin to choose right. They were sinning. They are not supposed to sin. So to him the answer was clear: Stop it!

I remember thinking about all the addicts I knew who were listening, and I felt sorry for them. His was a message I was sure they had heard before, and it had not helped them very much.

At the same time, I thought about both the truth and the error in what the preacher was saying. He was not wrong about addicts' choices being sin; virtually everyone agrees on that. But his statement that "people are free moral agents and responsible for their sin" is a loaded one.

The Bible does teach we are responsible and accountable for our sin. It is our problem and no one else's. But—and this would have been a surprise to the preacher—the Bible's message is much *more* devastating and convicting. For the Bible says not only that we are responsible for our sin, but also that we are powerless to keep from sinning. Think about that for a moment: we cannot change, and we are held responsible for not being able to change.

When we add in this other half—that we are responsible for that which we can't change—we find ourselves in much worse shape than the jail cell to which the preacher wanted to send people. In his thinking, people should go to jail for making bad choices, but they could avoid jail by choosing differently. And they could get out of jail by repenting and becoming better people. In the "powerless *and* responsible" view, you both go to jail and have no hope of getting out because you are unable to do better. And that is both what the Bible teaches and what any addict will tell you. No matter how many times someone with a compulsive behavior or an internal character problem tries to "just make better choices," it doesn't work. And they still find that they are held responsible for the reality of the problem and its devastating consequences: relational, health, career, etc.

In short, we are in prison or, as the Bible says, we are "slaves to sin." As Paul explains it, "I know that good itself does not dwell in me, that is, in my sinful nature. For I have the desire to do what is good, but I cannot carry it out. For I do not do the good I want to do, but the evil I do not want to do—this I keep on doing" (Rom. 7:18–19). That is a much more brutal message than the one the tough preacher was delivering.

But gracefully, the Bible does not leave us there. When we are thrown into prison with no chance of parole, when we are asked, "Anyone need a Savior?" the Bible gives us one. For it is exactly into that prison that Jesus comes and tells us he will break us out. This is good news indeed. When people realize that they are both powerless and responsible, they get serious about seeking help from outside themselves. Help has come in the form of the gospel.

The goal of this chapter is to give a few thoughts on how the problem of sin works in our lives and how the gospel is the answer to this problem in all areas of growth.

First, a Warning

When we talk about sin being a problem in the world of personal growth, we are not saying that a person's individual sin is the cause of all the struggles or problems he or she might have. All too often in the church, people are blamed for pain and struggles not of their own making. Job was a great example of this. He was not suffering because he was bad, but, it could be argued, because he was good. His losses were not his doing. In addition, people suffer because of the sin of others. We have all experienced long-standing suffering because of the abuse of another.

So, as we look at the subject of sin, let's first understand that everyone suffers and sometimes lacks growth for other reasons besides their sin. If we don't understand this, we may fall into the trap of blaming the hurting person, as Job's friends did. If we do that, we too will be "worthless physicians," and the best thing we could do would be to be "silent" (Job 13:4–5).

What Doesn't Work

Once upon a time, when Adam and Eve were in the Garden, they were free to do the right thing and avoid the wrong thing. But they did not do that, and now we have a real problem. Part of the problem is that we are *no longer free* to do the right thing, no matter how much we want to. Now, instead of freedom, we possess a "sinful nature" (Rom. 7:18). This nature has a passion for things that are not good for us ("Get behind me, apple pie!").

But it is even worse than that. Not only do we have a passion for doing those things that are against the law, but the law itself arouses in us a passion to do the very thing we shouldn't do (Rom. 7:8–10)! This is double jeopardy. We have the sickness, and the fact that we *ought* to be healthy makes us act out our sickness even more. Listen to the apostle Paul: "For when we were in the realm of the flesh, the sinful passions *aroused by the law* were at work in us, so that we bore fruit for death" (v. 5, emphasis added).

This is most easily seen in the young child who is told "no" for the first few times. Forbidding a child to do something seems to almost "make" him do it again. It is not as obvious with adults, but upon close inspection, it is as much present. We want to do what we shouldn't do.

This is one reason the three most common forms of

the "law" in Christian circles—harsh, angry preaching against sin with the injunction to repent, legalistic rules to keep people in line, and telling people (even lovingly) that the way out is to make better choices—fail so miserably with those caught up in something they can't stop. All of them assume a person's ability to choose rightly.

To compound the problem, these interventions produce in people the emotions of the law as well: guilt (condemnation), anger (rebellion), and fear. The Bible talks about our need to be freed from their effects (Rom. 5:20–21; 6:14; 8:1–2). So we can see that if we don't give people the whole gospel, we reap results we are not looking for: failure and bad feelings.

We have to do better than tell people they are wrong and they should do right. This is what the law does, and it is ineffective in changing people (Heb. 7:18–19; Rom. 8:3).

A Better Way

The Bible gives us a better way. As Paul says,

> What the law was powerless to do because it was weakened by the flesh, God did by sending his own Son in the likeness of sinful flesh to be a sin offering. And so he condemned sin in the

flesh, in order that the righteous requirement of the law might be fully met in us, who do not live according to the flesh but according to the Spirit (Rom. 8:3–4).

While the law (and all of our versions of it) cannot help, Jesus can. He replaces living by the law with living by the Spirit. This is the answer to all the problems sin can ever throw at us. Thus, while the standard is good and the need to make good choices is real, there is only one way to do that: Live according to the Spirit. This means to live according to a relationship and a process that empowers us (Gal. 5:16, 25).

So there we are again, back to dependency on God.

To change the areas we want to change, we must live according to the Spirit. (See chapter 5 for more on what this looks like.) Significant problems like addictions and other patterns of behavior do not give way to simple formulas such as "That is sin. I won't do that anymore." To achieve victory, we need to change fully in all of life as we commit to the life of the Spirit.

We cannot stop sin; we have to be *saved* from sin. And that means a much deeper healing process. In fact, as Jesus spoke of his mission, he said it just like that—as a mission of healing: "For the Son of Man came to seek and to save the lost" (Luke 19:10).

The word translated "save" in this statement is a word that actually means "healed" or "made whole." Being

141

saved from sin means being restored and healed at a much deeper level than we sometimes offer to people. People need more than just "Stop that!" They also need "and God and we will help you." The biblical process of overcoming sin provides a deep healing. Anything else will fall short.

So the Bible's commandment regarding sin is and always has been: Repent. The reality is, however, that "repent" means to have a total change of mind, to think differently—and that involves turning around our entire life, not just behavior. It means to think differently about sin, to see it as destructive and producing death. It also means to think differently about how we are going to deal with it.

"Repent" is not a shallow commandment. It is a total life change to the life of the Spirit and all that entails.

Rebellion

It is not just our inability to keep from sinning that gets us into trouble. We are sometimes very able to keep from sinning, and we choose not to. We rebel, as Adam and Eve did *before* they had a sin nature.

Even though we have the sin nature, at any given moment we do have control over some areas of our character, yet we choose not to exercise this control. There is no other word to use for this than *rebellion*.

Take the example of Sara and Joe.

Sara and Joe had had a rocky relationship for the five years they had been married. Not long after they got married, they began to argue intensely. Sometimes they argued over significant issues, but most of the time they argued over Joe's temper.

"I don't know what to do," Sara said, sobbing in my office one day. "I am not trying to control him or hurt him, but he lashes out at me in such a rage. I can't take it anymore." She said she was feeling herself grow cold inside, since she had been hurt so many times by him. I feared she might not stick it out.

Until then, Joe had tried to make his case to me about how difficult Sara was to live with and how his anger was justified. As he put it, "You would go crazy with her too." I would try to get him to look at her side of things, to no avail. But on this particular day, when the depth of Sara's pain showed itself, Joe gained a different perspective. In the Bible's words, he "repented." He changed his mind about his own behavior. He no longer saw it as justified, but as destructive and hurtful. He was hurting the person he loved and needed.

So Joe finally agreed to work on his anger. For a period of months, he and Sara would come back in when he was not able to control his anger. But these sessions were different from the previous ones. We were now working on his real anger problem and not something to be justified. He was going to a good support group, meeting with a prayer partner, and exploring with me the hurt and history behind his anger.

Slowly Joe changed as the "life in the Spirit" took hold. As Paul describes, he bore the "fruit" of the Spirit. He exhibited self-control, love, and patience (Gal. 5:22–23). More and more he became the loving husband Sara had desired.

One day, however, something happened. They had had a difficult weekend and had gotten into an intense argument. Sara was obviously wounded. When she described Joe's behavior, I was shocked, for I thought we had made more progress than that. My first feeling was one of empathy not only for her, but also for him, for his having been "caught in a sin" again (Gal. 6:1). I wondered what had snapped inside of him or what had overcome him.

As I listened to Joe, my empathy gave way to anger. Nothing had snapped in Joe. Nothing had overcome him. He was perfectly capable of not acting as he did—but he did anyway. What I saw was pure and simple "meanness." So I confronted him: "Don't give me any of this 'my issues came up' psychobabble. The truth is that you just chose to be mean instead of restraining yourself. This was a choice, and it is nothing but ugly sin."

I never will forget the look in Joe's eyes. He was caught. Then he got sheepish, shied away a little, and said, "You're right. I was mad, and I took it out on her. And that was wrong." I could see his spirit softening. He then turned to Sara and said, "I'm sorry." Sara softened as well. She accepted his apology, and they were able to go on from there.

It was a powerful lesson for him, and one that affected many of his other patterns of behavior. He learned that some problems in life are not about things we are "unable" to do, but about things we are "unwilling" to do. To rebel against what he knew to be right and loving felt good to him for the moment, but as is true of all sin, that was only for a moment. He paid the price in alienation afterward.

Sometimes we are unable to do what we are supposed to do. In those areas we need more work of the Spirit and need to flee the temptation and run to get help. But sometimes we do not use the abilities we do possess, and we willingly, willfully choose to sin (Ps. 19:13).

The solution to this is confession, remorse, repentance, making amends, and reconciliation with whomever we have hurt. There is a lot going on in the name of growth today that is just sin in need of repentance. One doesn't need the fruit of "self-control"; one just needs to exercise it.

No Excuses

I listened one day to a man talking about the affair he had had; we were working through its aftermath in his marriage. The affair had been devastating to his wife, and he seemed to have little insight into her feelings. In our sessions he caught a glimpse of the pain he had caused, but just when we were getting a little deeper into that, he changed the focus.

"All of this makes me sad for another reason," he said.

"What is that?" I asked.

"Well, if she had been meeting my needs, I wouldn't have had to go somewhere else to get those met."

I thought I was going to throw up. He basically said that his wife was responsible for his affair.

It had never occurred to him that he could have responded to her in a thousand ways other than by being unfaithful. He could have responded redemptively instead of destructively.

But then I had to become aware of something else. I have blamed others for my own behavior at times too. I have felt that familiar "Well, I wouldn't have done that if you hadn't . . ."

When Adam sinned and God came to confront him about it, Adam also responded as this man had. He said, "The woman you put here with me—she gave me some fruit from the tree, and I ate it" (Gen. 3:12). In one sentence Adam blamed both God and Eve. When God confronted Eve, she blamed the serpent.

Blame is part of the natural order of fallen humankind. We do not "own" our behavior; instead, we automatically shift responsibility. Blaming is human.

Death is human too. And the Bible says that to the extent we continue to explain our sin away, we will die. Blame keeps sin breathing and thriving in our lives.

Much blame goes on in therapy circles. People use their past—what happened or didn't happen in their growing up years—to explain away behavior. "I do that because my mother . . ." Getting to the roots of our behavior is very important. Many motivations or driving forces are not our fault. *But this does not mean that our behavior is not our responsibility.* If a man's father was mean to him growing up, and that man now hates and resists all authority, the father's meanness would explain part of his motivation. *But having that background does not explain why he chose to deal destructively with that hurt.* The only thing that can explain that is a fallen nature.

A spiritual response would be to submit that hurt and anger to the healing process and work it out without returning "evil for evil" (Rom. 12:17, 21). He would be getting healing for the hurt, getting resolution and forgiveness for the anger, and seeking reconciliation as much as possible with his father.

Sin Is More Than External Deeds

Too often we think of sin only in external terms. Jesus warned, "Now then, you Pharisees clean the outside of the cup and dish, but inside you are full of greed and wickedness. You foolish people! Did not the one who made the outside make the inside also?" (Luke 11:39–40).

The two examples above—the man who had an affair and my hypothetical example of a man who was hurt by a parent—show the importance of dealing with internal motivations. Unresolved anger and hurt can turn into bitterness or lust. Hatred for authority has probably ruined more careers than lack of training. And many other monsters lurk in the shadow of the human breast. Consider this list: "For it is from within, out of a person's heart, that evil thoughts come—sexual immorality, theft, murder, adultery, greed, malice, deceit, lewdness, envy, slander, arrogance and folly. All these evils come from inside and defile a person" (Mark 7:21–23).

Many illnesses, failures, addictions, relationship difficulties, and destructive behaviors originate in these motivators. As Jesus said, the fruit comes from the tree (Matt. 12:33–35). Looking inside ourselves and resolving the issues we find there is the key. We have to be made new from the inside out, and that begins with facing how ugly things are inside.

We all need a place where we can say, "You won't believe how sick I am! Let me tell you about this thought I had today." Then we can begin to clean up our insides.

From Morally Neutral To Morally Bad

What about the legitimate hurt in the soul? What if someone never deals with their hurt? What happens?

Unresolved hurt is going to do just that—hurt. The person who is brokenhearted and not getting healed is in pain. Often this person will do something to ease the pain. He may feel strong "cravings" for sex or food or alcohol to make himself feel better. He may feel driven to work and achieve at the expense of his loved ones. He may lust after material things, or he may strive for power to cover up his feelings of being small. Whatever the "drug of choice," unresolved hurt can tempt a person to sin. The hurt is not the sin. *The sin is the way that the person deals with the pain and emptiness.* It is a result of trying to meet a valid need in a sinful way.

The age-old story of the Bible is that we try to meet with our own idols the needs God is supposed to meet. We depend on man-made gods instead of the one true God. Meeting our needs our way is idolatry and never works. Our model is Jesus, who in his deprived state did not meet his needs through sin, but by dependence on God (Heb. 4:15).

Sometimes we fail to understand that deprivation can be the weak state that makes us susceptible to carrying out what the sin nature tells us to do. Therefore we need to respond to people's sin by looking beyond the sin nature to what is motivating and driving the sin. Some of what is behind "badness" is not so bad after all. It is a well of good needs and hurt and pain that people try to "medicate" in bad ways. This excuses none of the sinful answers we seek; neither does it excuse the partial gospels we give to people as answers to their sin. If we and the people we help are going to have victory, it has to come from all God has offered, and that includes taking care of the needs and the pains that are not connected to his life.

Avoiding Sin

In the meantime, temptation is still around. It does not go away, and we are not to sit idly and wait for it to subside while we are "getting well." The Bible has a strategy about avoiding it. Let's just remind ourselves of this strategy, as follows.

Pray

"Lead us not into temptation, but deliver us from the evil one" (Matt. 6:13).

"Watch and pray so that you will not fall into temptation. The spirit is willing, but the flesh is weak" (Matt. 26:41).

Flee and Escape

No temptation has overtaken you except what is common to mankind. And God is faithful;

he will not let you be tempted beyond what you can bear. But when you are tempted, he will also provide a way out so that you can endure it (1 Cor. 10:13).

Flee from sexual immorality. All other sins a person commits are outside the body, but whoever sins sexually, sins against their own body (1 Cor. 6:18).

Flee the evil desires of youth and pursue righteousness, faith, love and peace, along with those who call on the Lord out of a pure heart (2 Tim. 2:22).

We don't have to say a lot about these strategies, as they are self-evident. The problem is that a lot of people do not practice them.

How common is it to see people taking sin seriously enough to pray consistently to avoid it? And fleeing is drastically underrated. The Bible puts a huge emphasis on getting away from the temptation. It talks about fleeing it so we don't fall prey to it. While we are to resist temptation when we do encounter it, it is better not to flirt with it at all.

The principle is clear: Get away from tempting things *before* the temptation, not after. If you are not there, you can't be tempted. And when you find yourself in danger, don't just stand there and try to win. Instead, flee it— treat it as dangerous.

Remembering What Sin Is

Finally, we are tempted to forget what sin actually is. Remember the theology lesson in chapter 2? Sin is basically living independently of God, trying to be him. When there is a sin problem, we are likely to find problems in these areas:

- Independence—moving away from dependence on God as the source of life and trying to meet our own needs apart from God and his people
- Loss of relationship—isolation from God and others
- Boss—not submitting to God and obeying him
- Control—trying to control others or things we can't control, resulting in a loss of self-control and a failure to yield to God's sovereign control
- Judging—moving away from being real and experiencing life and others, and moving toward judging self and others
- Self-rule—trying to design life on one's own terms

Sin always appears as some form of independence from God. There is a deeper sickness that only humbling oneself before God can cure. In that one move, relationship is restored, and we once again become who we were created to be, humans and not gods.

One More Note

We can't deal with sin and temptation without confession and repentance. They are assumed in everything this chapter talks about, for it would be impossible to overcome sin and temptation without them. Confession and obedience are also part of repentance.

To love God means that we begin to obey him as well as do things his way. That goes a long way toward curing the problem of sin. But we need to mention that loving others is also part of the cure to many sins of the self.

Take the example of Dirk from chapter 4. Remember him? His weight was becoming a health danger, and so there was a real possibility that he might one day fall down with a heart attack. What I suggested to his accountability partner was to have Dirk stop thinking about his guilt and instead think about loving his wife and children. Think about what it would be like for small children to lose a father at a young age. Think about how daughters become promiscuous later, if they are looking for a father's love, or withdraw from relationships with men altogether. I asked him to have Dirk write a story about what his wife's and children's lives would be like without him for the next thirty years. Where would their income come from? Where would their guidance come from? What would happen to their lives?

The reality was that his sin of overeating would not only be a sin of the "self" that hurt him, but also a sin that could devastate the lives of others, all the way to the marriages of his children and their children. If Dirk could think of that, then love could constrain him just as our love for God constrains us also not to cause grief to him.

This is proven true by prison programs that get criminals eye to eye with the victims of their crimes. When the criminals see the pain they caused, they change. Love does its work where rules and commitment could not. That is why Jesus said that all the other laws and rules depend on love.

There are no victimless crimes, and in helping people with sin, the Bible affirms a strong message: Think of how your behavior is affecting other people, and that will motivate you to stop when rules won't. Remember, all the Law and the Prophets rest on the ultimate law of love.

CHAPTER 12

The Fruit of
SUFFERING
AND GRIEF

Physiologists tell us there is a reason I (Henry) am sore after I lift weights. I am sore because I have worked my muscles past their ability; I have stretched their capacity. After my workout, they rejuvenate and grow back to a higher level of development than before. I tear down to rebuild. And through the process of pain, growth happens. I hate it, but it is good.

The same God who designed and created our muscles designed and created our souls. God stretches our souls to grow them into something stronger and better. Sometimes he literally "wounds" and "heals" (Isa. 30:26), tearing down aspects of our character that need to be torn down and building up new aspects that we need in order to live as we were designed to live. So suffering can be good. It can take us to places where one more season of comfort cannot.

But some suffering is not a wound to heal. Such suffering inflicts evil on a person's heart and soul and is totally outside of God's desire.

I sometimes use this analogy when I speak: "If one of you walked out of this meeting and a guy with a mask walked up to you in the dark parking lot, took out a knife, stabbed you in the stomach, took all your money, and left you in an unconscious state, someone would call the police, and they would try to find the perpetrator.

"But if you left this meeting, drove down the street to the local hospital, and a guy with a mask came to you in a brightly lit room, took out a knife, cut your stomach open, took all your money, and left you in an unconscious state, you would thank him for helping you. One is a mugging; the other is surgery."

Suffering is a lot like that. There is therapeutic suffering, and there is destructive suffering at the hands of evil people. The key is to be able to tell the difference between the two and to apply the right kind of experience to each. Too often in the church those who have been "mugged" have been told that God is trying to teach them a lesson or that what they are going through is a result of their own sin or part of the growth process.

When life mugs someone, we need to give him or her healing, support, love, and comfort. We need to give strength and life support to those who are weak from things that have happened to them (1 Thess. 5:14). We are to "bear one another's burdens" (Gal. 6:2 NASB) and help each other through tough times.

Good Pain

Some pain is "good for nothing." Other suffering does have value. I call this "good pain." Dan is an illustration of how good pain can lead to growth.

Dan and his wife, Abi, were on the brink of divorce. When I met with them, I could tell this meeting was not his wife's idea. She said she had tried for years to reach him, to no avail. "Why would it be any different now?" she asked.

While Abi and Dan had had difficult times in the past—what I would call "bad pain," that is, pain that produces no change—this time *would* be different. For what they were both going through now was "good pain." This time Dan had been reduced to a place where his old coping methods no longer worked. The old Dan was dying.

Dan used to make up for the emptiness inside by performing, winning, and charming others into admiring him. One victory after another kept him afloat emotionally, but he always needed another fix. This time another fix was not coming, and he was trapped; the pain and lack of an internal life had caught up with him. All of the struts that had propped him up for years in his business had been taken away. And Abi, who had always been there to make him comfortable and secure without his relating or getting close, was no longer playing the placating role. So when she decided to leave him, Dan was left with his pain.

At first, Dan wanted me to make it all go away. I had to convert him to the idea that the only way "out" was "through." He was going to have to face some painful realities, and if he did that, he would never have to do it again. In the end, he would not be standing on the sands of performance, admiration, and status, but on solid ground.

So we went to work. Dan had to face the pain of his isolation. He had to face the anxiety of giving up all his controlling behaviors. He had to face the pain of the losses and hurts he had been hiding for all those years. He had to deal with strong underlying feelings of inferiority for which he was always trying to compensate with his performance.

It took a while, but in the end, Dan got to a much more "complete" state than if he had never crashed. He and Abi learned to connect at much deeper levels. For the first time he found more satisfaction in going on a walk with her than in making that next business deal. He also learned how to work in a saner fashion and to treat people better at work. The ways that he dealt with stress changed completely. As a result, he was able to go back to work and do it all very differently this time. He retained his talents, but he lost his former driven style.

When his life became a world of trials, Dan thought he was going to die. And he was right, just not in the literal sense. What would die were his old character patterns. It was God's design for those to die. As a result, Dan was resurrected into a new life, one that truly was "the life of God" (Eph. 4:18). In many ways, because of the death he died, he was alive for the first time.

This suffering is like that caused by the surgeon, not the mugger. Dan was not a healthy man, stabbed and left for dead and in need of a Good Samaritan. Dan was a sick, incomplete man in need of major surgery. And that is what God did in his life. In the end, Dan was put back together much better than before.

Stretching The Soul and Pushing Through

We all have coping mechanisms that cover up pain, help us deal with fear, enable us to cope with relational inabilities, and help us hold it all together. Trials and suffering push those mechanisms past the breaking point so we find out where we need to grow. Then true spiritual growth begins at deeper levels, and we are healed. Righteousness and character take the place of coping.

This kind of suffering is good. It breaks down and stretches the "weak muscle" of the soul and replaces it with stronger muscle. In this suffering, the prize we win is character (Rom. 5:3–5)—a very valuable prize indeed.

Maturity and completion are our goals. God says that we will not get there completely, but at the same time he tells us to press on toward those goals at all times (Phil. 3:12). This is pain that leads somewhere. Discipline does not seem joyful in the moment, but in the end it yields the peaceful fruit of righteousness (Heb. 12:11).

Every day a million Dans go through the kind of suffering he did, with no good end at all. They do not do it according to the will of God. They do not do it as Jesus did, being obedient all the way to death (Heb. 5:7–9).

In our lives, the death of certain aspects of character has to happen to get to the healing we need. So, as you are working through things in your own life or are helping others, have people look at their trials with the question, "What can I learn through this?" As James 1:5 says, have them look to God for wisdom to find out what steps of maturity and growth have to happen in their lives. If those steps are taken and completed, they will not have to take the same course again.

Bad Pain

Many times people suffer because of their own character faults. Then other people come alongside them and give them a spiritual pep talk about how God is with them in this testing. They usually frame the experience as the testing of an innocent person. "Keep the faith," these people say, "and God will reward you for persevering."

The problem is that these people don't tell the sufferers that the suffering is the fruit of their own character—from repeating old patterns and avoiding the suffering it would take to change them—and is of no value unless they see it as a wake-up call. This is false martyrdom. It happens when people lose a job because of performance issues and their friends and family see them as a "victim" of a bad boss or company. The friends would do well to say instead, "Have you thought about what is true about what they said? Have you thought about the fact that you are the common denominator with all of those 'bad' bosses?"

Bad pain is basically *wasted* pain. It is the pain we encounter as we try to avoid grief and true hurt that needs to be worked through. It is the pain of trying to get a person to love us or approve of us instead of facing the loss and moving on.

The Bible says, "As a dog returns to its vomit, so fools repeat their folly" (Prov. 26:11). Not facing the growth that we have to face always leads to further suffering—and the dynamics and symptoms and relationships usually get worse as time goes on.

How To Avoid Bad Pain and Embrace Good Pain

For those growing and for those who minister to them, the call is threefold. First, *do not refer to pain and suffering caused by character patterns as "growth pain."* It is not legitimate suffering. It is the fruit of a lack of growth.

Second, *help people own worthless pain so that it can be redeemed and turned into "good pain."* If a pattern can be owned, a pattern can be changed. But as long as we mistakenly see it as "legitimate suffering by a victim," nothing good can happen.

Third, *help convert worthless suffering into redemptive suffering.* In other words, help people resolve the issues. It is a very human trait to try to avoid the suffering of discipline and growth. We all do it. But the wiser we become, the more we value the pain of growth and despise the avoidance patterns in our lives. Help people face what must be faced and deal with it.

Peter: The Reluctant Sufferer

I was talking to a group of about a hundred experienced pastors and church-growth leaders in a training seminar. The topic for the day was how to help people grow spiritually in ways that affect real life. I began by giving them a hypothetical problem to solve.

"If you had to arm your parishioners with protection

from sin, how would you do it? What do you think would best equip them to not act out sinful patterns in their lives?"

Hands went up.

"I would teach them to pray."

"I would teach them to stay in the Word."

"Fellowship."

"Not placing themselves in temptation."

"Getting lots of support."

"Those are all good," I said. "Those are very important aspects of spiritual growth and becoming strong. But there is one aspect of spiritual growth that is particularly stated to be 'armor' against sin. Let me read it to you. It is from 1 Peter 4:1–2: 'Since Christ suffered in his body, arm yourselves also with the same attitude, because he who suffers in the body is done with sin. As a result, they do not live the rest of their earthly lives for evil human desires, but rather for the will of God.' What the Bible says is that having an attitude of embracing suffering will protect against sin. Let me tell you how that works."

What I told them was the story of Peter, the reluctant sufferer.

When Jesus said that he was going to suffer and die, it was Peter who told him there was no need for that (Matt. 16:21–22). Jesus promptly told him, "Get behind me, Satan! You are a stumbling block to me; you do not have in mind the concerns of God, but merely human concerns" (v. 23).

Jesus did not stop there. "If anyone would come after

Me, he must deny himself, and take up his cross and follow Me. For whoever wishes to save his life will lose it; but whoever loses his life for My sake will find it" (vv. 24–25 NASB).

Right in the midst of Peter's attempt to get Jesus to avoid the suffering he came to do, Jesus says that we must instead pick up our cross and die. Think of what this means in terms of growth.

Dan had tried for years to "save himself." Depending on his wit and abilities, he thought, would get him through and offer healing and salvation for life. Instead, Dan's attempts to avoid his pain promoted the growth of the cancers eating away at his soul, his career, and his marriage. And he was close to losing it all.

When Dan decided to pick up his cross and follow Jesus, he "learned obedience from what he suffered" (Heb. 5:8). As he faced his cross and the character patterns that needed to die, he found life as he had never known it before. He experienced salvation from his sin.

This is exactly what Peter found out. The same Peter who thought suffering and death should not be included in the plan later came to see suffering as *armor!* He came to see suffering as *protection* against sin. He came to see that if we go through the suffering we need to go through, then we are "done with sin" (or at least the sin that had to do with that particular growth step).

Picking Up the Cross

When Peter tried to get Jesus to forgo suffering, Jesus told us two things. One is that each person will have to pick up his cross; the other is that if a person tries to save himself, he will lose, but if he loses himself for Jesus' sake, he will gain his life. We have to identify with that cross. We have to be obedient to the suffering that will bring about holiness. We have to give up our own defensive and offensive attempts to save ourselves.

This is a very real part of how people grow.

Grief: God's Cure for What Isn't Right

Grief is the toughest pain we have to deal with. It is not the worst human experience (because it leads to resolution), but it is the most difficult for us to enter into voluntarily, which is the only way to get into it. The rest of our human experience just happens "to us." Hurt, injury, anxiety, alienation, and failure all break through, and we suffer. Grief does not "break through." It is something we enter into.

But its voluntary nature is not the only thing that sets grief apart from other kinds of suffering. The other difference is that *grief is the one that heals all the others. It is the most important pain there is.* This is why God calls us to enter into it voluntarily. It heals. It restores. It changes things that have gone bad.

Why is that? Why is it the "pain that heals"? Because grief is God's way of our getting finished with the bad stuff of life. It is the process by which we "let it go." And because of that, it becomes the process by which we can be available for new, good things.

The soul is designed to finish things. Just as a computer is programmed to run a particular path, so our soul is designed to go down the path of grief. Therefore, the Bible tells us: Be sad, and your heart can be made happy. Cry it out, and it will get out. It will be over.

The emotional investment in whatever was lost is being given up. We are letting go of what cannot be. Reality and our heart, mind, and soul have all come together. Tears are shed, and after many, many tears, we let go. "I will never have it, so I will let go of the wish." And like a leaf falling into a stream, it goes away. Then the heart is available for new things: new desires, new attachments, new hope, new energy, and everything that springtime brings. Winter has past, and it is the time for sowing new seeds of life.

We also bring to the new year the learning and understanding and experience that we learned in the old. Whether good or bad, what was lost was an experience, and from it we take understanding and wisdom for the rest of life. The process is complete, the person has grown, and the past is now the past and is not affecting the present, except in greater wisdom or the pleasant memories of a loved one who has passed on. The death experience has given way to the resurrection of a new life.

If Grief Is So Good for Us, Why Don't We Grieve?

If grief is the answer to so many of life's problems, why don't we just do it? If a sad face can make a heart happy, as Solomon wrote, why don't we have "sadness parties"? Well, we do. They are called funerals. They are gatherings where we can be sad and begin to process our grief. Funerals were a regular part of God's family practices with the children of Israel, and we have continued that practice, although we have limited funerals severely. The phrase "time of mourning" is one that appears several times in Scripture. The Israelites saw it as the right thing to do. And Solomon says, there is a time "to weep and a time to laugh; a time to mourn and a time to dance" (Eccl. 3:4).

We usually hold funerals only when someone dies, but we also need to grieve other things. The problem is that we don't often see those experiences as losses. So we stay in denial or the protest and bargaining phase for a long time, robbing ourselves of a new life.

Another important reason people cannot grieve the way they need to is that they lack resources. In short, grief is a letting-down and a letting-go. And we cannot let down and let go if we are not being held up. If there is not enough love to sustain us, both inside and out, then we cannot let go of anything, even something bad.

This is the answer to the age-old question that people ask every day: "Why doesn't he just get over it?" You don't throw away even rotten food in a famine. But if a new truck of food shows up, you can let go of the stuff that has died.

I wish that I had understood this process when I was younger. When I lost my dream of playing golf, I tried to find a new life without grieving for the old. But until I found the God who designed grief, I did not have losses—I *was* lost. Then, when I found the support and structure that God and his Body gave me, I could finally have losses. I could process them, and then I was found.

So in your own life and the lives of the people you help, grief may be the answer to your rut. You may be denying a reality lost long ago. You may be protesting something that will never come true. Maybe it is time to give it up. Maybe it is time for you to mourn so that your heart can be made happy again.

The Psalmist was right when he said, "Weeping may stay for the night, but rejoicing comes in the morning" (Ps. 30:5). The Bible affirms it and commands it, and science proves it to be true. There really is such a thing as "good grief."

CHAPTER 13

Waiting for the Harvest: TIME

Robin entered counseling with me (John) to deal with her marriage, her eating habits, and some depression. During my initial interview with her, I learned that she was a CPA who had earned her master's degree in business administration.

As you might have guessed, Robin was a very hard worker in spiritual and emotional growth. She took it seriously and faced many fears and problems.

One thing I began noticing was her perspective on how growth worked over time. For example, she discovered that many of her concerns had to do with a long-standing inability to grieve. When Robin found this out, she asked me, "Now that I know this, what do I do about it?" I told her, "You are going to have to learn how to let go of things, give up the demand to be so strong, and experience your weaknesses without running from them."

She thought about that and then said, "Okay, I'll have that done by next session. Then what?"

I started to laugh. I told her, "It's not like coming up with a project structure and implementing it into the business, hoping that it will have immediate results. Look at this more as how plants grow." Robin loved gardening. We talked about how she sets her plants in the right soil, waters and feeds them, makes sure the temperature and light are right, and keeps them safe from pests. She noted how you don't see results for a long time, then all of a sudden, life begins emerging from the soil.

Robin understood the analogy and said, "I suppose I need to get used to this time thing." And she did. She stopped expecting growth to be immediate, settled in, and eventually received the results she desired.

People will often enter the growth process with great hope and excitement and then, somewhere along the way, become discouraged that they aren't achieving results as soon as they would like. Someone is still struggling in a marriage; another is unable to open up emotionally to God and others; still another is unable to set appropriate limits; and someone else may be tormented by the pain of the past.

Spiritual growth facilitators may feel confused or guilty about the lack of fruit in the lives of the people in their growth group. They may wonder what they are doing wrong, or if they are letting the grower down, or how to even know what "too much time" is.

Spiritual growth should bring forth fruit of one kind

or another over time. If it doesn't, it could be a sign that something is breaking down along the way. The purpose of this chapter is to look at the role of the process as well as steps along the path of spiritual growth.

The Process of Time

So many growers expect that, if they read their Bibles and do the right things, they will instantly and permanently change. They are disappointed when this does not happen. They may feel God has let them down or they are doing something wrong, when in fact everything may be proceeding as God planned it. Time is a necessary ingredient of growth.

God originally did not include time in his plan, as he exists outside of time, in eternity. He experiences past, present, and future all at the same time. We, too, were created to live in an eternal state; however, when Adam and Eve sinned in the garden, God's wonderful creation was marred, and he knew that two things were necessary to fix the problem. The first was an atoning death to satisfy the requirements of his holiness. The second was a process of repair for his creation to be redeemed and healed from what it had brought upon itself.

This process we call time. Time takes the creation out of the eternal state, as quarantine takes a sick person out of the community. This is so that the disease of sin will not contaminate eternity. When the creation is healed of sin, time will be no more, as its job will have been accomplished. We will again enter the eternal state with God (Rev. 22:5).

The gift of time applies in the lives of individuals. When a person comes to faith in Christ, he is born again not as an adult, but as a spiritual baby. Like an infant, he must now enter the process of growth over time and receive the elements of growth that will one day mature him. This is what Peter means by our growing in salvation (1 Peter 2:2).

We aren't negating miracles by saying this. The Bible and our own experience show that God does do instant and marvelous things. And we need to ask for these, receive them when they happen, and thank God for them. At the same time, however, the norm taught in the Scriptures is a model for growth (Mark 4:26–29; Eph. 2:20–21; 4:15–16; Col. 2:19; 2 Peter 3:18). Teachings that only emphasize deliverances can create people who become dependent, not on God and his maturing ways, but on an event to heal them. Our suggestion for you is to work on the process and be open to the miraculous. God is for us in both ways.

So What Takes All The Time?

If you are a growth facilitator, you surely have heard the question, "Why is this taking so long?" Although you may understand the big picture of the growth process, it is often helpful for you and those you are helping to understand the specific ways in which time is a necessary part of growth.

Experience versus intellectual learning. Spiritual growth involves the whole person. All of our parts need to be exposed to God's love and healing: heart, soul, and mind (Matt. 22:37). This means that growth is much more than cognitively understanding or memorizing a fact, idea, or principle. If that were all that is involved, growth would be a much faster, cleaner, and simpler process. Simply learn a list, and you are healed.

Yet the Bible teaches that knowing truth is not enough (James 1:22–25). We need to add experience to our intellectual grasp of growth—what people call those eighteen inches between the head and the heart. Experience, by definition, takes time. For example, someone in your group may have an unloved heart. She certainly needs to be taught about the grace and safety of God and his care for her. But she also needs to experience God's care in her soul through his hands and feet. It may mean allowing her to experience fear and distrust without condemnation, so that she knows she is safe. It may mean letting her confess her pain and disconnection to others, and in turn receive the grace and tenderness from them that she can't manufacture for herself. All these events take time, much more than learning some facts. Yet they are essential.

Taking in grace and forgiveness. Of all the principles of growth, internalizing God's grace and forgiveness takes the most time. It is much more natural for people to try to earn God's love or to learn a habit or ritual. It is unnatural for us to live by grace and forgiveness.

I know a man in a growth group who, for the longest time, couldn't "get it" that when he failed, God wasn't mad at him. He would stay out of relationship with God and the group until he felt more under control. Then he would reemerge, thinking he was "okay." Finally he learned that those who loved him most wanted to know when he failed, so they could help restore him. But this reality took time, as the law had such a hold on him.

Repeated exposure to the elements of growth. Another reason we need time to grow is that it takes more than one "inoculation" for us to mature. A single lesson or experience is not enough. Growth often requires repetition to sink into our heart and character. The Bible calls this "practice": "Solid food is for the mature, who because of practice have their senses trained to discern good and evil" (Heb. 5:14 NASB). Psychologists refer to this as a learning curve.

Why is repetition necessary for growth? One reason is that we have many parts to our soul, and we may grow in one part but not another. A second reason is that we are often afraid of truth and light, and we will resist some reality about ourselves until we are safe enough to handle it. Add to this the reality that often we are on another path than God's in the first place. When we encounter growth principles, they may require that we turn around 180 degrees. And, just as turning a boat around in the water takes time, so does turning our soul around. It involves trials, risks, and failures.

Don't be afraid to have your group or ministry encounter the same principles again. They may need to soak things in more than once as they grow.

Internal versus external change. If you are helping others in the sanctification process, you are working with internal changes of heart and life. This change causes true character growth. It is from the inside out, not from the outside in. As hearts are transformed, they also transform the external life. But this takes time.

If you are working with a group and encounter a crisis—an addiction, an acting-out sin, a marriage breaking up, or the like—don't ignore it in favor of the internal issues. Rather, deal with both at the same time. Provide resources to help the crisis, such as people and places with specific experience in these matters. Simultaneously, keep working on whatever in the person's soul is driving these struggles. The internal work takes longer, but it has more lasting effect.

Determining Length of the Growth Process

Probably the second-most-asked question I encounter is, "How can I know how long it will all take?"

The first answer to this is: *It generally takes more time than you think*. Many of us get into the growth process hoping to get some quick answers and comfort and then resume "normal life." However, this is not God's way. For him, normal life is being in the growth process for life. Issues and struggles may and should change over time, but growth is not a season. Rather, it is at the heart of life itself: We "are being built together to become a dwelling in which God lives by his Spirit" (Eph. 2:22). So help your group get over the idea that because an issue has been resolved, they are "done." They may just be beginning.

Beyond that, several indicators can help people get a sense of time for their work.

Severity of the issue. People come to growth in varying stages of immaturity and injury. Generally speaking, the worse the issue, the longer the time required to resolve it. Expect the person with the worse battle to take longer.

Onset of the issue. As you get to know the people in your group, find out when their particular struggles began. Life has a way of continuing to injure already existing weaknesses, and it can become unclear where things started. Generally, the earlier the problem, the more time it will take to deal successfully with it.

Available resources. Although the work of spiritual growth is, at its heart, a miraculous act of God, it still requires resources, such as a healthy support system, a balanced church, good materials to study, appropriate leadership, and frequent meetings. The more resources available, the less time is needed.

As you help people grow, you may find that many

of them have spent a great deal of time addressing their weaknesses and struggles with little to show for it. Much of the time, they may not have had the right resources. Some may have been in a legalistic environment. Others may have lived in unsafe relationships. The availability of resources is a critical issue. Help your people unearth and use the good growth resources in your area.

Spiritual poverty. We already addressed this component in chapter 8, but we need to say here that, of all the factors, this one has the most effect on the length of time growth takes. Those who are truly aware of their need and hunger for God and growth will go and get it. And they will grow and resolve issues! Those without the hunger may have less severe issues, yet take longer to resolve them. For excruciatingly long periods of time, they may find themselves stuck in lukewarmness, blame, denial, or avoidance of pain.

Help people see the value of spiritual poverty in reducing the time needed for growth.

The Place of the Past

Time is also important in terms of the role the past plays in our growth. Here are some of the key principles.

An unresolved issue may mean that part of a person's soul is still "in the past." When a person struggles, he experiences some aspect of himself as split off and lost in an injured or

177

unloved state. It is as if the person grew up on the outside, but left a part of himself behind.

For example, a man I know suffered harsh criticism from his parents. When this man grew up and went to work, he could not tolerate criticism from his superiors. If his boss criticized him, he would immediately feel unloved, persecuted, and attacked. He would say to his group, "I feel like a little kid getting beat up." The part of him that needed security and approval was not adult, but childlike. This issue caused him many lost career opportunities.

Fortunately, the group was able to help him understand that his career problems had roots in his past. He came to the realization that God was present with him back as a little boy and now when he still felt the hurt. From his group he received the grace he hadn't gotten as a child. In time, he was able to receive criticism without losing a sense of love and security.

From this example I hope it is clear that we don't believe that for someone to work through their past, they literally have to go "into their past." This is impossible. All we have to work with is today (Heb. 3:13). It is more accurate to say that you help bring parts of the soul to grow past their immature or wounded state, and to mature and repair, so that they are integrated into the life of the present.

Think of all your group members as having parts inside them that are still in the past, whether or not they are aware of it yet, and help them see where they need to grow in these areas.

Most spiritual, emotional, and relational issues have a history. People do not generally have struggles out of the blue. Parenting problems, guilt issues, and faith doubts all have roots in the past. For empathy and perspective, know about your people's history.

You will see patterns emerge in people's lives. Often, understanding a pattern will help a person turn major corners in growth.

A single woman came to a growth group complaining that she couldn't find men of character to date. They were all controlling and self-centered. After some time in the group, one of the members said, "Charlene, you have a passive history. From your parents to your church to your boss to your dates, you have always let others decide your values and how you spend your time." This statement changed Charlene's life. She had let controlling men pick her. This awareness gave her much fuel to change.

Forgiveness requires a past. One of the most important elements of helping people grow is forgiveness (covered in greater detail in chapter 9). When we forgive, we cancel the debt of another, and we are free to live without the need to exact revenge on another. When we receive forgiveness, we experience God's freedom from our sin and guilt.

Some Christian circles teach that we are to forget the past and press on. They quote Paul's personal story of "forgetting what is behind and straining toward what is ahead" (Phil. 3:13) as an example. Yet, in that same passage, Paul talks about all the things in his past he had to deal with, such as self-righteousness, pride, and contempt for others (vv. 4–6). Help your people see the value of understanding their past both factually and emotionally as a key to forgiving.

Trauma. Often, as people feel safe in a growth context, their past will come back to them with a vengeance. The safety of love, grace, and structure makes it possible for them to bear what was previously unbearable. Old traumatic hurts, feelings, memories, and terrors may resurface, not as happening yesterday, but as if they are happening right now.

When trauma is re-experienced in a flashback, past and present are one. If you see that someone in your group is showing signs of this, hook her up with someone who has specific experience in that area. The goal is to help the person turn the flashbacks into memories that are not disruptive and frightening. Trauma problems are amenable to help, and people can resolve them and go on in their lives.

Growth for Life

The other day I met a woman who had been trained many years ago to disciple women in the basics of the faith and spiritual disciplines. She told me she had recently decided to mentor young women "on the side." She had been working with a young college student who was in turn training other young women in the faith.

"How's it going?" I asked.

"It's been very interesting," she said. "Nothing like I planned."

"What do you mean?"

"I was prepared to go through some materials on the basics of the faith, doctrine, the spiritual disciplines, and all of that other good stuff I was trained in, but she wanted to tell me about her life. About her struggles with her boyfriend and what she should do next. About her family and how her relationship with her mother had affected her choice of boyfriends. I was sitting there trying to figure out how all of this connected with following the Holy Spirit, praying, and the like. I know it does, and in many ways I know *how* it does, but I was just not prepared."

What she was describing is what all of us long for. We want to know our faith and the major biblical doctrines. We want to know what the Bible says about itself, God, and the spiritual life.

And we want to know what in the world these things have to do with our real lives. We want spirituality to be practical and real, from dealing with marital problems to overcoming difficulties reaching our goals, from dealing with depression to disciplining our children. We want God and real life to come together.

The woman I met expressed what we have tried to do in this book. We have taken an in-depth look at the major doctrines of faith. But we have also looked at real life in light of those doctrines. When you put God and his doctrines together with the struggles of your life, you will find that growth in both your faith and your life has no boundaries.

We encourage you to continue down this path. Get to know God better and take him and what you learn into every life situation you encounter. For then, we believe, you will realize Jesus' promise: "If you hold to my teaching, you are really my disciples. Then you will know the truth, and the truth will set you free" (John 8:31–32).